In a small town in Derbyshire, two middle-aged friends struggle to face up to the legacy of their shared childhood whilst also grappling with present-day relationships – with husbands, see and unseen, and a mismatched couple tied together by tragedy.

Lucinda Coxon's other plays include *Waiting at the Water's Edge* (Bush Theatre, 1993; published by Seren Press), *The Ice Palace* (Royal National Theatre, 1995; published by Methuen), *Three Graces* (Mercury Theatre, Colchester, 1995, while writer-in-residence at University of East Anglia). The plays have since been produced across Britain and the USA. She is currently under commission to South Coast Repertory Theater in Southern California. Screenplays include *Spaghetti Slow* (dir. Valerio Jalongo, 1995) and *Lily and the Secret Planting*. A third screenplay, *The Dyke and the Dybbuk*, is in development with British Screen and she is currently adapting Rosamond Lehmann's *The Echoing Grove* for the BBC.

A Methuen Modern Play

Copyright © 1997 by Lucinda Coxon
The right of Lucinda Coxon to be identified as the author of this work
has been asserted by her in accordance with the Copyright, Designs
and Patents Act, 1988

First published in Great Britain in 1997
by Methuen
Random House, 20 Vauxhall Bridge Road, London SW1V 2SA

Random House Australia (Pty) Limited
20 Alfred Street, Milsons Point, Sydney, New South Wales 2061,
Australia

Random House New Zealand Limited
18 Poland Road, Glenfield, Auckland 10, New Zealand

Random House South Africa (Pty) Limited
Endulini, 5A Jubilee Road, Parktown 2193, South Africa

Random House UK Limited Reg. No. 954009

Distributed in the United States of America
by Heinemann, a division of Reed Elsevier Inc.
361 Hanover Street, Portsmouth, New Hampshire NH 03901 3959

A CIP catalogue record for this book is available
from the British Library

Papers used by Random House UK Limited are natural, recyclable
products made from wood grown in sustainable forests.
The manufacturing processes conform to the environmental
regulations of the country of origin.

ISBN 0 413 71990 1

Typeset by Wilmaset Ltd, Birkenhead, Wirral
Printed and bound in Great Britain by
Cox & Wyman Ltd, Reading, Berkshire

Lucinda Coxon

Wishbones

Methuen Drama

Wishbones was first performed at the Bush Theatre, London, on 11 June 1997. The cast was as follows:

Audrey   Amelda Brown
Gwen   Madeleine Newton
Colin   Gawn Grainger
Alan   Kevin McMonagle
Mary   Jane Hazlegrove

Directed by Simon Usher
Designed by Anthony Lamble

Characters

Audrey, *forty-seven*
Gwen, *forty-seven*
Colin, *forty-nine*
Alan, *thirty-nine*
Mary, *seventeen*

All born in Derbyshire. They still live there, with the exception of Audrey who has spent the last twenty-odd years abroad.

The action takes place in a Derbyshire town, Abu Dhabi and Ostia, present day.

Note

'Well-dressing' is the custom of decorating springs and wells with pictures made from fresh flowerheads and petals. It is a practice all but unique to Derbyshire.

Act One

1

The upstairs landing of **Gwen** *and* **Colin**'s *house in Derbyshire.* **Gwen** *is in her dressing-gown. It is a cold night, but* **Gwen** *is hot. Her cheeks burn.*

Gwen *is looking at a large flat parcel propped against the wall. The parcel is wrapped in brown paper and tied with string. She is troubled by it.*

She looks out of the landing window. Outside, the moon turns the snow an icy blue.

Gwen This – cold . . . and yet . . . look at me . . . sweatin cobs. This moon . . . big as a sun.

In a darkened villa in Abu Dhabi, **Audrey** *opens a slat in the venetian blinds and light pours in. She immediately closes it again.*

There is the faint sound of a sprinkler playing on the grass outside.

Gwen Sucking all the water in us to it.

Audrey I think – when I allow myself to think – the thing I miss the most of all's the water.

Gwen Terrible hard stuff, the water here. It's all the limestone.

Audrey You could taste the calcium in it.

Gwen Splash it on your face and it's drier than when you started!

Audrey Bones and teeth. Bones and teeth.

Gwen Makes your skin grow old before its time.

Audrey Hairs on your chest like bars of iron. That's what our dad used to say.

Gwen Enough of that.

Audrey Your dad.

Memory.

Colin *appears on the landing, barely awake.*

Audrey *opens out a blue aerogramme, takes up a fountain pen, starts to write.*

Colin   Love?

Gwen   Mm?

Colin   Can't y'sleep?

Gwen   No.

Colin   What y'doin?

Gwen   Thinkin.

Colin   What about?

Gwen   Nothin much.

Colin   Must be somethin.

Gwen   Just thinkin, that's all.

Beat.

Colin   Right.

Beat.

Gwen   I'm confused.

Colin   What about?

Gwen   I don't know.

Colin *puts his hands on her shoulders, but she shrugs them off.*

Gwen   Don't mither me.

Colin   No.

He looks out of the window with her, then:

Snow's settled. Back t'bed?

Gwen   In a minute.

Colin   Gwen...

Gwen   I promise.

Colin *gives in.*

Colin   I'll warm your side up ready.

Colin *leaves.* **Gwen** *is alone again. She sits down by the package.*

Gwen   I want to cry. Why do I want to cry? I haven't got anything to cry about...

Gwen *rests her head against the package.*
Audrey *reads what she has written.*

Audrey   'They catch the falcons in the desert, sell them with their eyes sewn up. You replace the eye thread with a burqa, protect your wrist with a manqala. These birds are fierce. Yet in under a month you can train them. They will answer to their names. You fly them on a line at first, and when the line is cut ... they stay within its former radius. Tame ... loyal ...'

Why ...?

She slowly crumples the aerogramme.

Between memory ... and hope, there is a place where you can live and bide your time. Sit quietly, and listen to the rhythm of your own insides. A kind of hibernation, I suppose. And it doesn't keep you young, or anything like that. But it stops your parts from getting worn. Why, I could slip my heart out now and turn it in my hand, as shiny as a girl's ...

As the lights fade down, the parcel could almost be a headstone, **Gwen** *lying on a grave.*

2

A harsh bright bell rings as Alan enters his dark and dingy shop.

The bell also wakes **Gwen.**

Alan *rolls up the blind on the door, turns the sign to 'Open'. Looks out at the day.*

Gwen *gets up, goes off, still sleepy, unsteady.*

Alan *approaches his desk. Stops. Turns the old swivel chair with his hand, round and round and round and round. This action takes all the time it needs.*

The bell rings again and **Colin** *hurries in, carrying the package.* **Alan** *starts to surface – it is later now – he's not sure how much later.*

Colin   How do!

Gwen *follows, lagging behind.* **Colin** *sets the package down carefully.*

Colin   Sure you're all right now?

Gwen   I'm fine.

Colin (*to* **Alan**)   We've brought you something in t'have a look at, but I'm on a double yellow. You'll sort her out will you . . . ?

Alan   I'll try . . .

Colin   Smashing. So, Gwen, exactly how you want it, yes . . .

Gwen   You're going t'get a ticket . . .

Colin   I know . . . b'bye.

He kisses **Gwen** *quickly on the cheek, waves and leaves, the bell clanging as he goes. A moment's silence.* **Gwen** *draws breath to speak, but can't quite manage.* **Alan** *waits.* **Gwen** *lays her hand on the package. The room is hushed for an uncomfortable length of time.*

Alan   You've brought me something.

Gwen   It's an old thing.

Alan   Right.

Alan *waits.* **Gwen** *shows no sign of wanting to unwrap the parcel. Then:*

Gwen   Can you work wonders?

Alan   What is it they say? 'The impossible takes a little longer.'

Gwen   I wasn't sure if you were open. Usually you can see a light. I drive past sometimes with Colin and I can see a light.

Alan   Didn't notice how late it was.

Gwen   No. Creeps up on you this time of year. The dark.

Alan   Yes, it does. So . . .

Gwen   Oh – there's no hurry for this. It's just to get an idea.

Alan   Of what could be done.

Gwen   And how much.

Alan   Right.

Gwen   It's a present, you see, for my birthday. T'have it repaired.

Alan   Restored. I don't repair, I restore.

Gwen   Oh . . . restored. I . . . we . . . mostly have modern things. But my husband's father passed on lately, so money came. Now this is not an antique. Don't think that. It's just old. I mean you'll probably laugh, say 'what d'you want that old thing for?'.

Alan   I doubt it.

Gwen   No. It's nice t'have some old things, wouldn't you say? I mean modern things are nice, but they don't last. Whereas this . . . it's old as the hills!

Alan   Mrs . . . ?

Gwen   Gwen.

Alan   Gwen. Are you going to let me have a look?

Gwen   Oh. Yes. Of course.

Alan *advances on the package. Crouches down by it, forcing* **Gwen** *away. He gets a sense of it through the paper.*

Alan   When is your birthday?

Gwen   End of Feb. But it doesn't have to be ready by then.

Alan   No problem.

Alan *starts to pick at the knots in the string.*

Gwen   Very end – twenty-ninth.

Alan *registers the information.*

Alan   Leap year baby.

Gwen   Why my husband likes to make a fuss. Well no – he likes t'make a fuss, full stop. Christmas, birthdays – looks forward f'months, then's disappointed b'the time they arrive.

Alan *takes out a penknife, cuts through the string.*

Gwen   This last Christmas was the first without his dad, so that was tricky. No one t'pull the wishbone with. I don't like. Somebody always loses. Makes me feel sorry for the turkey. Bit late by then, I know . . .

Alan *starts pulling the paper away from the package.* **Gwen** *looks away. Her eye lights on a photograph pinned to the wall by the desk.*

Gwen   This your son?

Alan *stops. Looks round.*

Alan   No.

Gwen   Oh. Only it says 'Bradley and Son' . . .

Alan   I'm the son.

Gwen   Your dad's business.

Alan   Great-grandfather started it.

Gwen   Eyes like yours.

Alan   My nephew. Steven.

Alan *tries to continue unwrapping the package.* **Gwen** *points to the swivel chair.*

Gwen   He's sitting in that chair. There's that clock in the background . . . a quarter to five.

Alan   He worked here for a while.

Gwen   But then had better fish to fry.

Alan   No, then he died.

Gwen   Oh I'm . . . I'm sorry . . .

Alan *tears the paper from the package.*

Alan Used t'do the upholstery for me. I farm it out now. Chap down the road. He's very good. Let's see what you've got here.

He concentrates on the ornate wooden frame, painted grubby white, with its tattered upholstery centre. He turns it, examines the back, perplexed.

Gwen Is it not worth bothering with? Colin says we do it up or chuck it out, it can't just sit in that back room for ever, and I can see his point . . .

He pries the upholstery free in one corner. A tearing sound. **Gwen** *flinches.*

Alan I'm just not sure what it is.

Beat.

Gwen It's a bedhead.

Alan Right.

He shakes his head.

And that's what you want it restored as?

Gwen What else?

Alan What you've got here is an old overmantel mirror. It's a nice one too, but some fool's taken the mirror out, padded the centre. Years ago, b'the look of it.

Gwen *is amazed, bewildered.*

Gwen I had it on my bed when I was little . . .

Alan Well it had a different life before that. Needs taking apart, starting from scratch. Was it always painted like this?

Gwen I've a feeling that to start with it was green, a pale sort of peppermint green . . .

Alan *scrapes away at a corner, flaking off the paint.*

Alan Rafferty's motor car back here. All have to come off.

But he looks up to see **Gwen** *distressed, fanning herself.*

Gwen I'm sorry, I . . . you've . . . you've thrown me . . .

I'm just . . . I'll be fine in a . . .

Gwen *looks as though she might actually faint.*

Alan   Here . . .

He quickly pushes the swivel chair over for her, horrified. She sits.

Let me get you a . . .

Gwen   No.

Alan   . . . glass of water or something . . .

Gwen *shakes her head.*

Alan   I've some pop . . . what d'you call it . . . Coke in the fridge . . .

Gwen   No . . .

Alan   Are you sure . . . ?

Gwen   It's just getting . . . my . . . breath . . .

Alan *stands back as* **Gwen** *works to regulate her breathing, get back on an even keel.*

Gwen   I get so hot . . . so hot . . .

She loosens her coat, breathes. It's a real effort to get on top of this. After a while, **Gwen**'s *calmer, but clearly debilitated by the flush.*

She breaks the silence.

Will you talk to me?

Alan   I'm sorry . . . ?

Gwen   Will you . . .

Alan   What?

Beat.

Gwen   I need to think. About the thing. The bedhead.

Alan   Mirror.

Gwen   Why stir all this up now?

Alan   Sorry?

Gwen We slept in it for years, Audrey and me. Siamese twins . . . Used to lie there, tell stories. Her dad was in the navy, so she knew about faraway places. They buried him at sea. He didn't die at sea. Died in hospital at Plymouth. But they took him out and tipped him over.

Then she was an orphan.

After the funeral she said to me, 'Have you noticed how in all the best adventures, people don't have parents?' Brave. And yet she clung, to me. And mine.

It doesn't seem right to touch this without asking her.

Alan So . . . ask.

Gwen She lives abroad now.

Alan Phone.

Gwen We were sitting on the landing stage, watching the river run by. She said 'We're off to Aberdabby.' I said 'Kath Allsop went to Wales last week, it rained the whole time.' Abu Dhabi. I never imagined she could go so far.

Alan People move around these days.

Gwen We've not.

Alan No.

Beat.

Look, Mrs . . .

Gwen Gwen.

Alan I shut at five. So?

Gwen I don't know why I came here.

Alan Y'husband wants t'get you this done up for your birthday, right?

Gwen Yes.

Alan But I've confused you.

Gwen Sort of.

Alan *runs his hands over the piece.* **Gwen***'s going to need firing up.*

Alan   Let me tell you what I'd do in your shoes. Strip the wood back to nothing and polish it up. Get some really good glass in, bevelled edges. It's a lovely thing, this. Let it live again.

Gwen   It wouldn't be the same.

Alan   No, but this isn't whatever you want it to be. It's got its own story. A record o' whoever made it and used it. What's this mirror seen? Where was that tree before it got carved up? Don't you want to know about that?

Alan's *hopeful but* **Gwen** *can't rise to it.*

Gwen   I want to take it home with me but it's too heavy to carry.

Alan   Right.

Gwen *starts fastening her coat.*

Gwen   I'm sorry.

Alan   You can leave it here, pick it up another day.

Gwen   I might change my mind, get it done like you say . . .

Alan   Just let me know.

Gwen   And I really am sorry.

Beat.

Alan   Talk t'your husband, see what he says.

Gwen   Will I help you wrap it up again . . . ?

Alan   You're fine.

Gwen   Right. Then thank you for your time.
You will look after it – ?

Alan   You'll talk to your husband?

Gwen *nods, the deal struck, hurries out into the dark rainy evening. The bell clangs behind her in the now quiet room.*

Alan *covers the bedhead over with paper, moves it out of the way. He goes to the door, turns the sign around – 'Closed'. He looks out into the street. Outside, a young woman –* **Mary** *– whirls around and around* *on the spot, her arms outstretched.* **Alan** *is disturbed to see her. He watches for a couple of seconds, then draws down the blind.*

Mary *whirls on, the sound of the rain and the traffic getting louder. Car headlights dance across her spinning form.*

3

The upstairs landing at **Gwen** *and* **Colin**'s. *Night.*

Gwen   And so . . . the thing is, Colin . . .

the thing is that . . .

that night after the day we'd dug a deep hole in the earth, and laid your father in it . . . that night, when everyone was gone, you . . .

gone . . .

you took off your black suit, your tie, and then we . . . then we . . .

She cannot say it. She becomes angry.

And afterwards, you lay there in me still. Nothing I could do. You lay there, leaking into all the corners of me.

I couldn't move, how could I? – your face, all wet with tears.

I held my breath, not wanting to let anything in.

I didn't want for there to be a child.

She steadies, her confession out.

And later on, a month or two, I thought there was a child. And that was like the whole world held its breath. I didn't want a thing to suck the goodness out of me. Trapped there inside, to grow and grow, and turn me inside out with being born.

But it was something else . . .

The relief of it floods through her.

A part of me that wouldn't breathe again . . .

So, inside now, I'm quiet . . . Full of the sound of no sound . . . Of no accident waiting to happen.

And it sounds as though a debt is cleared!

And some nights, like tonight, the sound is deafening, and I can't sleep – don't want to sleep. I want to listen now it's quiet.

And as the heat runs through me, on a night like this, I pass through the double-glazing, over the patio, into the night. Cross the fields and down to the landing stage.

She is at the landing stage now.

No more sitting watching life flow by! I'm out of the river's frozen shallows, pulled towards the warm. Portugal, Algeria, the Mediterranean, Suez. Red Sea, round Saudi. And here: Arabia. The Persian Gulf.

She 'sees' someone standing before her.

And through the heat haze, there she is. We are, again. We shimmer. And she laughs, as if to say, 'I always knew you'd come.' Even after all the times I never did, she wouldn't give up hope of me. And I look at her – all smiles. And I say – 'Wait . . .' I say . . . 'You don't know what I am . . . have done.'

Her distress gives way to consolation.

And she says, 'no . . .' – her finger to my lips . . . She says: 'It's gone.' She says: 'No need.' She says: 'It doesn't matter now . . . Let's start again . . .'

4

Weeks later. Day dawns on the landing stage. **Gwen** *is there, as at the end of the previous scene. Colin hurries on with a jacket for her, excited.*

Colin   Y'left this in the car.

He holds it out for her.

Gwen   Why are we here?

Colin   It's a surprise! Slip it on now. And cover your eyes –
I mean it.

He hurries off again. **Gwen** *pulls on her jacket, then covers her eyes.
Moments later,* **Colin** *enters with a cake ablaze with candles. He
sings:*

'Happy birthday to you . . . happy birthday' – y'can look
now – 'to you . . . Happy Birthday dear Gwennie . . .' – Gwen,
look –

Gwen *finally looks at the cake.*

Colin   ' . . . Happy birthday to you!!!'

He hands **Gwen** *the cake. She blows out the candles.*

D'you make a wish?

Gwen   No.

Colin   I'll light them again . . .

Gwen   It's silly.

Colin*'s disappointed, but recovers.*

Colin   Whatever.

He spreads a car rug on the ground. Sits.

Let's cut it then.

Gwen *settles beside him, cuts two big slices.*

Colin   Cheers.

Colin *tucks into his cake.*

Gwen   You don't have t'take the whole day off, y'know.

Colin   They'll rub along without me. Hey – today, Gwen, I
was thinking – Alton Towers! You and me on the big dipper!
What d'you say?

Gwen   It's for kids . . .

Colin   Be a laugh!

Gwen   Is this grass damp?

Colin   I don't think so . . .

Gwen   You don't want to make yourself bad.

Colin   I'm fine.

Gwen   And getting behind at work.

Colin   One day!

Gwen   I want y'to promise me something.

Colin   Open your cards . . .

Gwen   I want y'to promise you'll go into work.

Colin   But I told you . . .

Gwen   No, Colin! I want you t'go in.

Colin *gives in.*

Colin   OK. Fine. I'll go in.

Gwen   I don't want you getting yourself out of sorts.

Colin   No.

He takes a deep breath and fishes something out of his jacket pocket. He pushes the small package towards her.

Happy birthday my love.

Gwen *opens the package. A wristwatch.*

Gwen   Oh – it's . . . it's lovely . . .

Colin   You like it?

Gwen   Yes, it's . . . but you shouldn't have . . . I've got this one . . .

Colin   I wanted you t'have a good one. You've had that other years.

Gwen   Still goes though.

Colin   Come on . . .

Gwen *undoes her watch.*

Gwen   I'll wear it f'best.

Colin   No! Everyday! What are we waiting for Gwen? We should have the best every day!

The new watch is fastened on **Gwen**'s *wrist.*

Colin   Now that's lovely.

Gwen   Yes.

Colin   You look lovely. You do like it?

Gwen   Yes.

Colin   Let's open your cards.

Gwen *nods. She seems troubled by the new watch.*

Colin   Have I done it too tight?

Gwen   I'll get used to it.

Colin *almost says something. Changes his mind. Draws a sheaf of envelopes out of his jacket pocket.*

Colin   Well then.

Gwen *looks through the envelopes, doesn't find what she's looking for.*

Colin   Nothing from Audrey, I'm afraid.

Gwen *misses a beat, then ploughs on, starts to open her cards.*

Gwen   'Ted, Sally and the girls', that's nice.

Colin   Shame after all this time.

Gwen   What is?

Colin   Whatever's happened. No letter.

Gwen   I never send her one.

Colin   S'pose not.

Gwen   You never even liked her.

Colin   She didn't like me.

Gwen   Y'know, I was right.

Colin   What?

Gwen   This grass. It is damp.

Colin   Gwen!

Gwen   What?

Colin   What's the matter?

Gwen The grass!

Colin No!

Gwen Why are y'shouting at me on my birthday?

Colin I'm not . . . I just . . . I'm sorry, Gwen . . . Look praps it's me. It's mebbe me.

Beat.

Gwen It doesn't matter.

Colin No, it's your birthday, I shouldn't have.

She touches him.

Gwen It's all right.

Colin *savours the warmth of* **Gwen**'s *hand.*

Colin Yeah. Yeah it's fine.

Gwen *looks at her watch.* **Colin** *is pleased, then:*

Gwen Better get going or they'll think you're not coming in.

Colin Right.

He considers, then starts something new:

What will you do today, Gwen? All on your own.

Gwen I've plenty t'get on with.

Colin Good. That's good.

Gwen Don't worry about that.

Colin No. Love?

Gwen Mm?

Colin Y'might think t'give that chappy a ring.

Gwen Who's that then?

Colin The furniture repair man.

Gwen Restorer. He doesn't repair, he . . .

Colin I called him last week.

Gwen *is cornered.*

Gwen   Why did you do that . . . ? I told y'it wasn't ready . . .

Colin   Y'said it wasn't finished. He's never even started.

Gwen *busks hopelessly.*

Gwen   Has he not . . . ? Well I'll get onto him about that.

Beat.

Colin   You'd only t'say, Gwen.

Gwen   Say . . . ?

The weight of **Gwen**'*s lie sinks in.*

I . . . I just . . . I thought you'd be disappointed. I thought y'heart was set on it.

Colin   My heart is set on you, Gwen. You.

Gwen   Oh God . . .

Colin *moves to hold her. She resists.*

Colin   Come on . . .

She reaches out to him, then pulls away.

Gwen   Don't be nice to me, you'll get me upset . . .

Colin   So get upset.

Gwen   I don't want to.

Colin   Yes . . .

He folds his arms around her and she responds for a moment, but then pushes him away.

Gwen   No.

Colin *backs off.*

Gwen   You won't give up on me will you, Colin?

Colin   Why would I do that?

Gwen   I don't know.

Colin   Oh Gwen. Come on, I'll drive you back.

Gwen   I can walk. Nice day. Never know when we'll get another.

Colin   Let me drive you.

Gwen   Really.

Colin *waits but* **Gwen** *won't look at him. He starts to walk away.*

Gwen   Col!

She holds out her hand.

My old watch. Could I? Just t'keep.

Colin *takes it from his pocket, hands it over.*

Colin   Happy birthday, Gwen.

Gwen   Yeah.

She lifts her sleeve, shows **Colin** *her new watch.*

It is lovely!

Colin *walks away without looking back.* **Gwen** *holds her old watch to her ear, listens to the ticking, closes her eyes and lets her mind wander. Steadies herself in the rhythm.*

5

The landing stage. Weeks later. **Gwen** *stands with the watch to her ear.* **Alan** *enters, sees her, hesitates. He's reluctant to stop here, but concerned.*

Alan   Hello?

Gwen *surfaces. She recognises him.*

Gwen   Oh . . .

Alan   Miles away.

Gwen   I was.

Alan   You want to be careful down there, you know. Some funny types round the park.

Gwen   Thanks. I will.

Alan   Anyway. So long as you're right.

Alan *goes to set off again.*

Gwen   I say – I'm sorry about the mix-up over the . . . y'know.

Alan   Don't worry about it. Although if you could pick it up some time. I get a bit short of space.

Gwen   Course.

He's about to leave again.

Out for a walk?

Alan   Not exactly . . .

Gwen   No?

Alan   Came to see about some hydrangeas. Gardener lets me have 'em for the well-dressings.

Gwen   You do the well-dressings?

Alan   In the family. Always have.

Gwen   But that's not till summer.

Alan   End o'May. It's April now.

Gwen   April . . . already . . . ?

Alan   On Wednesday.

Gwen   Oh . . . we used t'play at the wells when I was a girl. Throw ha'pennies in. Never hear 'em hit the bottom.

Alan   They're deep all right.

Gwen   Had nightmares about falling down.

Alan   Got grates over now.

Gwen   Ought to block 'em up.

Alan   Those wells g'back t'Roman times. Never know when you might need 'em. Anyway . . .

Alan *looks as though he might be about to go.*

Gwen   I wrote to my friend.

Alan   Your . . . ?

Gwen   Audrey – the one I . . . I told you about her. She never wrote back.

Alan Sorry. Praps moved.

Gwen Maybe.

Alan And letters take a while to get places.

Gwen Feb twenty-ninth, I wrote. She missed my birthday. First time ever. I never bothered with it, keeping in touch. But when I didn't hear from her, I thought . . .

Gwen *shrugs.*

Alan It might get there yet.

Gwen You never know. I do hope . . . that nothing's happened. All these years she's been away, but I don't know what I'd do without her. Silly, isn't it?

Alan *really wants to go.*

Alan Look, I'm walkin back into town if you want t'walk with me.

Gwen *considers.*

Alan You don't want t'hang around here.

He moves uncomfortably down towards her, extends his hand.

Gwen I'd like that. Thanks.

Gwen *takes his hand and he helps her up the landing stage step.* **Alan** *shepherds her away and out of the park.*

Mary *appears out of nowhere, watches them moving away. She holds up her hand in a still, silent wave, willing them to turn and see her. But they don't. Her hand falls. She watches until* **Gwen** *and* **Alan** *are out of sight, then turns her attention to the river.*

6

A small room off the Methodist Church Hall. A hot day at the end of May.

Gwen *leans over a large table with a clay-filled board on top of it. Her hair is gripped back off her face. She concentrates hard, embedding tiny* *beech cones in the clay on the board. Her back aches, but she works on through the conversation.*

Alan *brings in another box of beech cones. He puts it down and inspects* **Gwen**'s *work, adjusting it here and there.*

Alan   How's it coming?

Gwen   Not bad.

Alan   Bit boring this stage.

Gwen   No, no I'm not bored.

Alan   I'll see if I can get someone off the side panel of Suffer Little Children t'give y'a hand.

Gwen   More cones?

Alan   Not sorted I'm afraid.

Gwen   I'll go through them.

Alan   I'd best pick up those bits from round the corner.

Gwen   Sure.

As soon as he's gone, **Gwen** *stops, stretches out her back. She looks at the work she's done so far. Adjusts a couple of cones, goes back to work.*

Mary *appears in the doorway.* **Gwen** *registers.*

Gwen   Oh ... have you come t'help?

Mary *seems distressed. She's bewildered and dead serious.*

Mary   Are you in trouble?

Gwen   No ... I just ... I thought y'might've been sent.

Mary   I was looking f'someone but he's not here.

Gwen   Alan?

Mary   How d'you know that?

Gwen   Y'said 'he' and there's only one. Is it important?

Mary *considers.*

Mary   Yes.

Gwen   He's popped out t'pick up some clippings f'the lamb.

Mary   Lamb?

Gwen   Of God. Next door, table in the corner. Lady in the lilac pinafore. There's a place clips poodles gives us the white bits for 'em. And what's left over comes in handy f'the beards on the elders. He won't be long.

Mary *checks the doorway, nervous, then casts an eye over* **Gwen**'s *work.*

Gwen   What d'you think?

Mary   It's spelt wrong.

Gwen   Don't say that!

Mary   'As Pants the Heart' – you've missed out the 'e'.

Gwen   No, no. It's 'hart' as in deer. 'As pants the hart for cooling streams when heated in the chase.' It's a deer, y'see, being hunted. Look, there's its hooves . . . its face . . .

Mary   No eyes.

Gwen   Y'do those later with coffee beans. They stand out better. It's only the main outlines y'use cones for.

Mary *feels the row of cones.*

Mary   Not gonna rain then.

Gwen   No?

Mary   Cones're all open. They shut up shop when rain's coming.

Gwen   Learn that at school?

Mary   Not at school.

Gwen   Oh. Why don't y'stop a minute and do me the eyes?

Mary   I can't.

Gwen   Doesn't matter if y'get it wrong. Y'just puddle the clay flat again'n'have another go. I picked it up in no time.

Mary   He wouldn't like it.

Gwen   Alan? But you and him're friends.

Mary Not friends.
Related, sort of. Are you his friend?

Gwen Not exactly...

Mary I saw you with him...

Gwen Oh?

Mary At the shop, then in the park. You don't remember
me.

Gwen No.

Mary *looks back at the doorway.*

Gwen Do me the eyes. Go on. It's right in the middle
where it catches my back. I'll show you the picture he's done
of what it's supposed t'look like in the end... when we've got
all the petals on'n'everything...

Mary Go on then...

Gwen Fantastic! And when it's up on the well at the
weekend, you'll be able t'say 'I did that. Without me that
deer'd never've escaped cos it wouldn't've been able t'see
where it was going.'

Mary Just show me the picture.

Gwen Right.

Gwen *unrolls a huge sheet of paper with a coloured drawing of a hart
flanked by stylised trees. The words 'As Pants the Hart' across the top.*

Mary He did this...

Gwen It's a lovely job.

Mary *inspects it closely.*

Mary Little holes...

Gwen Where he...

Mary ... pricked the pattern on the clay. Why does he do
it?

Gwen It's tradition.

Mary Why?

Gwen   Well, y'decorate the wells t'say thank you, for the clean water. For it still being there.

Mary   So it's a kind of magic, this? To keep the water coming.

Gwen   I don't know about that . . .

Mary   It works.

Gwen   It's more a way of saying that you don't take things for granted. You know they could change. You do it every Whitsun.

Mary   What is Whitsun?

Gwen   Whitsun . . . D'you know, I've no idea, which is very bad of me. You'll have t'ask Alan when he gets back.

Mary   I'm off now . . .

Gwen   I thought you were going to . . .

Mary   Sorry.

Gwen   Should I tell him . . . ?

Mary   No, no . . . forget it . . . bye.

Gwen   I'll know you next time.

Mary   Will you?

Gwen   Course.

Mary *lifts her hand in a parting gesture, but as she moves to the doorway,* **Alan***'s there, filling it. He is shocked.* **Mary** *seems terrified.*

Alan   What's this?

Mary *can't speak.*

Alan   Get out.

Mary *doesn't move.*

Alan   I said out!

Gwen   This is possibly my fault . . .

Alan   She knows whose fault it is.

Mary   I'm sorry.

Alan   Don't want t'hear it.

Mary   Y'weren't at the shop.

Alan   I said I don't want t'hear...

Mary   I thought something had happened...

Alan *moves from the doorframe, points the way out, refusing to look at* **Mary**. *She opens her arms to him, willing him to make eye contact. He does, then looks away.* **Mary** *continues.* **Alan** *meets her gaze, stares her out, willing her to leave.* **Gwen** *can only watch as the two stand locked in silent combat.*

Suddenly, **Mary** *races towards* **Alan** *and launches herself at him, wraps her arms and legs around him, clings on. He struggles with her for a moment, then manages to fling her to the floor.*

Alan   God Jesus fuck she's bloody mad the girl's completely bloody...

He brushes at his clothes, trying to shake off the memory of her. **Gwen** *moves to help* **Mary** *who's curled in a ball on the floor.* **Alan** *collects himself.*

God, she just... well, you saw her... how she... how she just...

Gwen   I saw.

Alan   I'm sorry... I... she scared the living... you know...

Mary   I'll go now.

Alan   Good.

Colin *arrives.*

Colin   What's cracked off here?

Gwen   It's a family thing...

Colin *heads straight for* **Mary**.

Colin   Dear, oh dear.

Alan   There's been a misunderstanding...

Colin   Come on, now. Don't cry, suck your orange.

He produces a clean white hanky, gives it to her. **Colin**'s *arm slips easily around her. He lifts her, curls her into him.*

Have a good blow . . .

Mary   I'm not really crying.

Colin   I can see that.

Mary   I landed on my elbow.

Colin   Your funnybone! Well never mind, you're young, you've plenty of bounce left in you. Listen, you don't want t'worry about family squabbles and I'll tell you f'why. Do you know about Einstein's theory of relativity?

Mary *shakes her head.*

Colin   Well you should, because it proves scientifically that time passes more slowly when you're with your relatives. Come on now.

He leads her to the table.

What's this then?

Mary *looks at* **Alan.** **Alan** *looks away.*

Colin   Never mind, laddo, I'm asking the questions.

Mary   She did it.

Gwen   You were going t'help me though, weren't you?

Mary   I don't know.

Colin   What kinda dog is it?

Mary   No, it's a hart. Without an 'e'.

Colin   Oh I see. 'As Pants the Hart . . .' Fantastic. And what were you goin't'do t'help?

Mary   Maybe his eyes. She said to.

Colin   Gwen did?

Mary *looks to* **Gwen.** **Gwen** *nods.*

Mary   Gwen.

Colin   Now what's your name?

Mary *looks to* **Alan** *again. A silence in the air before he answers for her.*

Alan   Mary.

Mary *nods to* **Alan**, *filled with emotion. He turns away.*

Colin   Mary, Mary, quite contrary, mm?

Mary *can't take her eyes off* **Alan**. **Alan**'s *not going to look back.*

Mary   I have t'go.

Mary *hands back* **Colin**'s *hanky, now damp and screwed up.*

Colin   Keep it. I've plenty more.

Colin *nods.* **Mary** *takes the hanky back. Looks at* **Gwen**, *then slips past* **Alan** *and out of the door.*

Beat.

Alan   She told y'she's family?

Gwen   Related, she said.

Alan   She killed our Steven.

Colin   That little girl . . . ?

Alan   As good as. Now she's after being the death of me. You saw her.

Gwen *and* **Colin** *can't comment.*

Alan   Look . . . can we just . . .

Colin   Forget it.

Gwen   Yes.

Alan   Right.

Alan *nods, leaves.* **Colin** *and* **Gwen** *collect themselves.*

Colin   So much for Saint Alan.

Gwen   Don't be like that.

Colin   He'd knocked her for six!

Gwen   He's a very nice man! He must have his reasons.

Colin   She's only a thing and a thank you!

Gwen   You're not supposed t'be here for another hour.

Colin   I know that . . .

Gwen   Come t'snoop?

Colin   What?

Gwen   Just when I was getting somewhere! Everything I do, you take over.

Colin   I'm sorry you feel that way, Gwen. I'd come t'tell y'something.

Gwen   What?

Colin   No, no. I wouldn't want to interfere.

Gwen   Has something happened?

Colin   I'll be in the car.

Gwen   Colin!

But he's on his way out. Calls back:

Colin   Your Audrey's come home.

Gwen   She's come . . . ?

But **Colin***'s gone.*

Gwen *pulls off her overall, throws it aside. Smooths down her clothes. She is dazed by the news.*

7

Audrey *and* **Gwen** *stand on the upstairs landing of* **Gwen** *and* **Colin***'s house.* **Audrey** *looks out.* **Gwen** *watches her.*

Gwen   So this is my . . . . . . where I live.

Audrey   Even this far out of town you can see the river.

Gwen   We're quite high up.

Audrey   You've changed your hair.

Gwen   Have I?

Audrey   I like it.

Gwen   Changed itself. I pull the grey ones out.

Audrey   Do ten grow back?

Gwen   I don't think so. Look at you. Are you . . . ?

Audrey   What?

Gwen   Real.

Audrey   Feels like it.

Gwen   I thought about you.

Audrey   I know that now.

Gwen   I thought a lot. Like living with a ghost sometimes.

Audrey   I'm flesh and blood, Gwen. More than I could do with in some places.

Gwen   Oh, no. Lovely and slim still.

Audrey   After the boys? I wish.

Gwen   I can't imagine it. Y'look just . . . like yourself.

Audrey   Thank you. For your card.

Gwen   I can't believe you're here.

Audrey *turns back to the window.*

Audrey   Come and look out with me. Point out all the old things.

Gwen *hesitates, then approaches* **Audrey** *by a few steps. Then she joins her at the window, and they both look out into the night.*

Audrey   I got lost in a one-way system coming here. Thought I'd never make it. Round the same great roundabout time after time.

Gwen   You drive.

Audrey   Don't you?

Gwen   No.

Audrey   Will I teach you?

Gwen   It's a bit late.

Audrey   I think you should learn.

Gwen   I could get a car.

Audrey   Of course you could. I saw where the Palais used t'be.

Gwen   Long gone now.

Audrey   The time we had no money for setting lotion. Fixed our hair with sugar water.

Gwen   Mum's idea, that.

Audrey   The wasps buzzing round us all night.

Gwen   Set like concrete.

Audrey   But looked fantastic.

Gwen   Look but don't touch!

Audrey   And sucking on strands of it when we walked home.

Gwen   In trouble for getting back late.

Audrey   Because we had to wait till the wasps were asleep.

Gwen   It's nice to smell you. Smell your smell.

Gwen *puts her arms round* **Audrey**. **Audrey** *holds her.* **Colin**'s *voice calls from downstairs.*

Colin (*offstage*)   If the grand tour's over it's G and Ts all round!

The two women break apart.

Gwen   We better go.

Audrey   We better had.

Gwen   I thought you'd forgotten all about me.

Audrey   No you didn't.

Gwen   No. But I thought maybe something had happened.

Audrey   And now it has.

Gwen   Yes.

Audrey   You made it happen.

Gwen   Yes.

Audrey   It'll all be all right now.

Gwen   Will it?

Audrey   I promise.

Gwen   Can you do that?

Audrey   What do you think?

Gwen *looks* **Audrey** *up and down, smiles. They laugh.* **Colin** *enters with a tray and the laughter stops. Music plays softly in the background. We are in* **Colin** *and* **Gwen**'s *front room.* **Colin** *hands out drinks.*

Colin   I don't suppose y'see a lot of this out your way – alcohol.

Audrey   Actually, the rules are different for foreigners.

Colin   Well cheers anyway. And I'd like to say how welcome you are.

Colin *raises his glass.* **Audrey** *hesitates, then follows, then* **Gwen**. *Music dominates for a moment.*

Audrey   Lovely. Puccini.

Colin   It's the Music from Morse actually.

Audrey   Ah.

Colin   So where are you stopping?

Gwen   She's in a hotel.

Colin   Bit impersonal for you.

Audrey   That suits me.

Colin   Oh. This weather'll be about right for you too, I s'pose. Cos we're on our knees with it aren't we? Not set up for it, see. Wrong sort of clothes – shirts and ties! It's the ones your way got it right with the old flowing robes.

Audrey   And the air-conditioning.

Colin   Ah, yes. And that's my line these days. Heating engineer.

Gwen   Plumber! That's what *you* always say.

Colin   Little business, specialising in conditioned environments. Anyway – Abu Dhabi, Audrey. I'm trying t'get a picture of it in my head. It's hot, dry.

Audrey   Humid.

Colin   And the landscape . . . ?

Audrey   Desert, far as the eye can see.

Colin   Does that get boring?

Audrey   You develop a new perspective. Learn to read its variety.

She tells **Gwen***:*

The Shamal comes . . . out of nowhere. You're never ready, you can't be. The dust flying and the winds driving faster than your car. And it moves the mountains. Grain of sand by grain of sand. A long time ago, the nomads measured it. It's true. Once you know these things, not boring at all.

Colin   The . . . the local women, they're all in the yashmaks'n'that?

Gwen   Too many Turkish Delight ads!

Audrey   It's called a burqa.

Colin   See! And they all wear them do they?

Audrey   Mostly yes. There are bare-faced women, but they're mostly Iranian, or Omani, Baluchi.

Colin   All the time, or just when they're out and about?

Audrey   The burqa goes on when their periods start, stays on till they stop. Our age. Then they can show their faces again. In between, it comes off for your husband or for prayers.

Colin   You know, I'd love to visit. Wouldn't you, Gwen?

Gwen   I suppose . . .

Colin   Here we go . . .

Gwen   I like it at home.

Audrey   That's nice.

Colin   I've got a freebie holiday come September – one of the big boiler companies. One-day trade fair in Rome, Italian seaside for a week. Ostia. She doesn't want t'go.

Gwen   It's not straightforward as that.

Colin   Doesn't want t'leave the house.

Gwen   There's been burglaries.

Audrey   Couldn't someone stay here for you?

Gwen   Yes, but . . . you know what these seaside places are. You've seen the brochure, you've been there. I can't see why you should have to travel all that way t'find out something y'already knew.

Audrey   Italy's not far.

Colin   That's what I said!

Gwen   It's not the point . . .

Audrey   But if you don't want t'go, I don't see why you should.

Colin   Well – t'see the sights, and just . . . how other people live.

Gwen   I can imagine.

Colin   What about Abu Dhabi, you must wonder what it's like there . . .

Gwen   I know what it's like.

Colin   You can't do.

Gwen   I can.

Colin   Anyway, it'd be too hot for you.

Gwen   That wouldn't bother me.

Colin   Y'hate it too hot.

Gwen   I do here, but if I was there, I'd be different.

Colin   How would you?

Audrey   ˙How?

Gwen *thinks.*

Gwen   My clothes would be different. I'd wear a jacket, that fits just so. With a little peplum so it flatters all the bumps.

The others laugh, but **Gwen** *is serious.*

It's a pale, pale colour, with little pearl buttons. And it's linen. I'm in Rub' Al . . .

She looks to **Audrey** *for a prompt.*

Audrey   . . . Khali.

Gwen   Khali. The Empty Quarter. The yellow sand, rippled like water. All steep slopes and sudden shadows. And I'm thinking how it looks just like desert, yet there's plants still because some of them bury their roots so deep. And I'm thinking how the sand is full of seeds that lie dried up for years till it rains, and then all of a sudden, they come to life. And I'm thinking maybe tomorrow I'll go to the oasis, to Al Ain to see the camels race. Or out to Sadiyat Island to the beach. But I mustn't be late back – for cocktails at the Club. And I've to pop into Gray Mackenzie on the Corniche and pick up a few bits and bobs. Things to remind me of home. Ritz crackers and Dairylea cheese! I don't have to worry how much I buy, because I've got a car. I don't know what kind . . .

She looks to **Audrey.**

Audrey   You've got a Subaru.

Gwen   Oh. Is that good?

Audrey   It's ideal.

Gwen   That's all right then. I told you I could imagine.

Audrey *nods.* **Gwen** *is exhilarated,* **Colin** *amazed.*

Colin   Bloody hell, Gwen!

Gwen   I know all your letters, see.

Audrey   I see.

Colin   Ah – except you haven't picked the kids up from school yet ...

Gwen   Oh ... ?

She looks to **Audrey**.

Audrey   You don't have to, they're away.

Gwen   Aha!

Colin   Far away?

Audrey   Wiltshire.

Colin   You live over there and your kids live in Wiltshire?

Audrey   That's right.

Colin   How old are they?

Gwen   Colin ...

Audrey   It's all right.

Colin *(to* **Gwen***)*   What?

Audrey   Sam is at college, Jon has one more year at school. It's a good place.

Colin   I'm surprised you don't miss them ...

Audrey   Did I say I don't?

Colin   No.

Gwen   No.

Audrey   Out there, we're not allowed to own anything, only visiting. I didn't want the boys growing up like that.

Colin   Sure. Just seems odd, I mean, when you decided t'have children you must've thought ... about coming home maybe, I don't know ...

Audrey   No. You don't. I should be off.

Colin   Sorry ...

Audrey   I'm on a different clock, you see.

Gwen   But you've only just got here ...

Audrey   Only wanted to show my face.

Colin   I've gone on, look I'll take myself out of the way . . .

Audrey   No really, I'm tired.

Colin   But you've hardly had any time together . . .

Gwen   Here you are, Colin.

She hands him her empty glass, shutting him up. He collects **Audrey**'s *too.* **Gwen** *walks a little way towards the door with* **Audrey,** *shutting* **Colin** *out.*

How long will you stay?

Audrey   Depends.

Gwen   You mightn't have t'go back for a while?

Audrey   Back . . . ?

Gwen   Home . . . there.

Audrey   Oh, I'm not going back.

Gwen   Not . . . ?

Audrey   Didn't I mention that?

Colin   No.

Audrey   So you see, there's no hurry. See you tomorrow, Gwen. Lunch?

Gwen   Yes . . . course . . .

Gwen nods.

Audrey   Colin.

Colin   Bye . . .

Audrey *leaves. The room settles again.*

Colin   Crikey. She's a bit . . .

Gwen   What?

Colin   Y'know.

Gwen *watches through the window after* **Audrey.**

Gwen   You frightened her away.

Colin   I didn't mean to . . .

Colin *gives up, takes the glasses out.*

Gwen   You've done it again . . .

8

Mary *squats on the lower steps of the landing stage, peers down into the river. She 'dips' between herself and her reflection.*

Mary   Dip, dip, dip, my blue ship, sails on the water, like a cup and saucer, o-u-t spells out.

The reflection is 'out'. She splashes the water.

Go on. Out.

She splashes again but the reflection returns. She takes **Colin**'s *hanky from her pocket and lays it over the reflection's face.* **Mary** *becomes aware of* **Gwen** *behind her. Panics. Dabbles the hanky in the water.*

I was just washing this.

Gwen   I see.

Mary   Couldn't get into the bathroom this morning.

Gwen   Are there a lot of you?

Mary   Yeah.

Gwen   Brothers and sisters?

Mary   Some.

Gwen   How many?

Mary   I couldn't say. A lot.

Gwen   Must keep your mum busy . . . ?

Mary   I don't live at home. I'm in a B & B. I want t'get this clean so I can give it back.

Gwen   I don't think Colin's too worried about it.

Mary   It's got his inital on it.

Gwen   I know. I embroidered it.

Mary   You did that?

Gwen *nods.*

Mary   It's nice. You're good at things like this, aren't you? I'm not.

Gwen   Probably never tried.

Mary   Don't need to. I'd be rubbish.

Gwen   You might not.

Mary   I would.

Gwen   Only one way t'find out.

Mary   People say that, but it's wrong.

Gwen   You're right. It's a stupid thing t'say.

Mary   Will he come t'the fête tomorrow, y'husband.

Gwen   I expect so.

Mary   Praps I can give it to him then?

Gwen   If you like.

Mary   It won't make him cross? I'll keep out of everyone's way. Don't worry.

Gwen   I'm not worried.

Mary   You should be. After yesterday. Did he tell you? Is that why you've come? T'see where it all happened.

Gwen   No . . . I'm meeting someone. What all happened here?

Mary   What he told you.

Gwen   He didn't tell me anything much.

Mary   What?

Mary *waits – she wants to know.*

Gwen   Steven.

Mary   He died. I had to make a choice. Of who to save. Him or me. I chose me.

Gwen *pieces it together.*

Gwen   Steven drowned?

Mary *nods.*

Gwen   But it's not your fault if you were a better swimmer.

Mary   I wasn't in the water. Didn't he say?

Gwen   No.

Mary   Oh well. Never mind.

Gwen   No. Life goes on.

Mary   Not mine.

Gwen   Everybody's.

Mary   Mine's got stuck.

Gwen   You need something to take your mind off things.

Mary   I don't want my mind off things.

Gwen   Brooding does nobody any good.

Mary   I don't deserve any good.

Gwen   That can't be, Mary.

Audrey *arrives.*

Gwen   Hi ...

Audrey   Hi.

Gwen   Audrey, Mary.

Mary   You from round here?

Audrey   Used t'be. My aunt's house was just up the road. Where Carpet World is now.

Gwen   She's been away.

Mary   Why've you come back?

Audrey   I don't know ... Cos you always do in the end.

Mary   I did.

Audrey   There you go then.

Mary   Why did you live with your aunt?

Audrey   I was more often at Gwen's mum's.

Mary   Where was your mum?

Gwen   Mary . . . !

Audrey   She died. When I was born. My dad couldn't look after me on his own. So I came up here.

Mary   D'you miss her, your mum?

Audrey   What you never had you never miss.

Mary *thinks, floats her hanky on the reflection.*

Mary   I'd like something I never had.

Audrey *looks to* **Gwen.**

Mary   It's OK, I'm going now.

Mary *wrings out the hanky and hurries off.* **Gwen** *and* **Audrey** *watch her go.*

Gwen   Don't ask.

Audrey   I won't. Am I late?

Gwen   I'm maybe early. Couldn't concentrate.

Audrey   What have you been doing?

Gwen   We're putting the petals on now. Blue hydrangeas for the water.

Audrey *smiles.*

Audrey   It's all still here.

Gwen   Yes.

Audrey   I somehow thought if I wrote every year it might be. Twenty-five years.

Gwen   Twenty-four letters.

Audrey   Yes.

Gwen *looks out over the water.*

Gwen   River's low. Y'can see t'the bottom at the edges here.

Audrey *reaches out, runs her index finger down* **Gwen**'s *spine.* **Gwen** *freezes.*

Audrey   I draw a snake upon your back.

Gwen   Oh.

Gwen *is relieved.* **Audrey** *holds up her fingers.*

Audrey   Which finger did it?

Gwen *picks one.*

Audrey   How did you know?

Gwen   Good guess.

Audrey   They say good guessers shouldn't get married.

Gwen   Try again – best of three.

Audrey   I draw a snake upon your back . . .

Gwen   You've left Philip.

Audrey   Which finger did it?

She wiggles her fingers. **Gwen** *chooses.*

No! I draw a snake upon your back . . .

Gwen   Audrey . . . ?

Audrey *wiggles her fingers.*

Gwen   This one.

Audrey   Yes. You're better when you don't think too much.

Gwen   I don't blame you. I think marriage makes you old.

Audrey   If you stick with it long enough.

Gwen   No, I mean it makes you . . . stand still.

Audrey   So it's time to start moving again.

Gwen   For you.

Audrey   Us.

Gwen   I've got Colin.

Audrey   Here.

Audrey *takes a green half-bottle from her pocket.*

Gwen   Gin!

Audrey   Why not?

She takes a swig. Holds out the bottle to **Gwen**.

Gwen   My petalling'll be all skew-whiff. There'll be whirlpools in the cooling streams.

Gwen *drinks*.

Audrey   What's kept you and him together?

Gwen   No one else'd have me!

Audrey   That isn't true.

Gwen   You don't know what I'm like.

Audrey   Don't I?

Gwen   What I'm like now.

She drinks.

I have thought about it. Being without him. I don't want anything bad t'happen to him. I mean I'd be devastated . . . But if he could be removed . . . just temporarily, in limbo somehow . . . I'd like t'know how it'd be. Is that bad?

She drinks again.

Sometimes I imagine . . .

Audrey   What?

Gwen   Terrible things. Things I'm ashamed of. I'm at his funeral. I look fantastic. And I'm upset – I mean I am really upset. I can make myself cry just thinking about it. But I do think about it just the same. I can't help it. Is that bad, d'y'think? And I feel so . . . free!

She gives **Audrey** *the bottle.*

He's not always dead . . .

Audrey   Oh good.

Gwen   Sometimes he just leaves me. I fall apart. Go t'pieces. It's a terrible tragedy . . . but I quite enjoy it.

Audrey   D'you think he would?

Gwen   What?

Audrey   Leave you.

Gwen   Where would he go?

Beat.

Other lives . . . you wonder.

Audrey   Dream.

Gwen   I suppose.

Audrey   But never try to make it real?

Gwen   I might not like it.

Audrey   No.

Gwen   It's like . . . the other day in Sainsbury's, there was this woman and she was very . . . I don't know . . . stylish. And in her basket – things I'd never buy. But you could see how she could throw them together and make a super dinner. Basil, she had – in a pot, still growing. And tomatoes, and some kind of cheese . . . I mean, things we could afford, but I would never think. And then she had these other things, like little oranges – tiny-weeny ones, and the more I looked at this woman and her basket, the more I had to know what they were.

It was nearly my turn at the checkout, but I snapped. Like a mad thing, I went. Found them. Kumquats they're called. I bought a bagful.

Audrey *nods.*

Gwen   And do you know, I could feel how that woman felt inside, having those kumquats in my basket.

And do you know something else? They were disgusting. Turned your mouth right inside out. I tried one on Colin. His face puckered up like a dorothy bag. Had them in a bowl on the side for a while. They went mouldy in the end, and I threw them away. But in that twenty minutes in that queue, I learned something it had taken that other woman her whole life to pick up.

Beat.

Audrey   Gwen, I'm not sure things work like that. If a thing's going t'be any good you've got t'put your whole self in.

Gwen   You make it sound like the hokey cokey.

Audrey   We could do that, Gwen. Put our whole selves into something.

Gwen   Could we?

Audrey   When I breathe now, I feel it fill up my ribs. This bone fit to burst. I realise, for years I've been breathing too shallow.

Gwen   I don't know if I've got it in me . . .

Audrey   You wrote to me.

Gwen   Wish you were here.

Audrey   Now I am. I see you, Gwen, hear your voice – and I know where I am. I'm happy.

Gwen   I want you to be happy.

Audrey   You make me happy.

Gwen   I shouldn't be too much longer.

Audrey *registers.*

Audrey   OK.

Beat.

Is it how you thought?

Gwen   I didn't think.

Audrey   You must have.

Gwen   In your mind it's different. This gin's making my head swim.

Audrey *takes change from her pocket.*

Audrey   Let's make a wish – like we used to! But not in the wells. In here, so we can see them hit the bottom. So we know they'll come true!

Gwen   I don't know . . .

Audrey   Go on. Just a penny! Let's take our chances,
Gwen!

She sorts out a penny for **Gwen**.

Audrey   Ready?

She makes eye contact with **Gwen**, *making sure the magic's strong.*
She waits. **Gwen** *holds her coin, ready to throw, then pulls back:*

Gwen   You go ahead ... I'm not sure exactly what t'wish
for yet.

Audrey   That's wise, Gwen. Y'need t'be sure. I'm sure.

Audrey *closes her eyes then flicks her penny into the river. They watch*
where it splashes and sinks.

Gwen   It's in the shallows.

Audrey   Look how the sun catches it.

Gwen   Minnows.

Audrey   'Minnows.'

Audrey *smiles.*

Gwen   What did you wish for?

Audrey   Not telling. Now you.

Gwen *takes her penny. She's about to throw, then:*

Gwen   I'm nervous.

Audrey *waits.* **Gwen** *almost throws again, then:*

Gwen   I can't.

Audrey'*s disappointed.*

Gwen   Sorry.

Audrey   Well ... there's no hurry.

Gwen   No.

Audrey   I can wait. I'll drive you back.

Gwen   No ... if I'm here on my own for a minute, I might
make my wish.

Audrey   I'll see you later then.

Gwen   Yes. I mean maybe. I might have to work late.

Audrey   Call me.

Gwen   Bye-bye.

Audrey *crosses her fingers.* **Gwen** *returns the gesture and* **Audrey**
leaves.

Gwen *stares down into the water. There's* **Audrey**'s *penny.*
Gwen's *worried by it. She wants it. She's got to get it. She leans a long
way out off the landing stage, soaking her sleeves, but it's too far.*
Gwen *leans further, soaking her shirt too.*

*Increasingly desperate, she pushes out as far as she can. She's breathless
now, her entire torso in the river. She finally grips the coin but can't raise
herself back up. Starts to panic, flail as* **Mary** *returns.* **Mary**'s *upset
to see* **Gwen** *in the river, angry.*

Mary   What are you doing?

Gwen   Help me up . . . can you . . . help me . . .

Mary *pulls her up.*

Mary   What were you doing in there?

Gwen   Nothing . . . I . . . I . . . thought I saw something.

Mary   What?

One of **Gwen**'s *flushes has a grip.*

What did you see!

Gwen   Nothing . . .

Mary   Why were you looking?

Gwen   It was nothing.

Gwen's *obviously suffering.* **Mary** *relents.*

Mary   You mustn't go in there.
You're so hot. Come'n'sit in the shade.

She helps **Gwen** *over.*

Are you all right?

Gwen   I'm fine, yes . . . just . . .

Mary *pulls a dock leaf, strokes it along* **Gwen**'*s cheek.* **Gwen**'*s helpless.*

Mary   Here. Dock leaf. These are good when you're hot. You mustn't look in the river, Gwen.

Gwen   No. OK.

Mary *goes back to the river, floats her hanky.* **Gwen** *undoes her blouse, obviously still very distressed.*

Mary   It is lovely what you've done here. So neat.

She lifts the hanky, looks into the river.

Do you know the story of the greedy dog?
He carried his bone to the river and looked in, saw another dog with a bone. And he thought the other dog's bone looked nicer than his. So he snapped at the other dog to get the other bone, and he dropped his own in the river.

There was no other dog. There is no other bone.
This is the place where I drowned my little girl.

Gwen *looks up.*

Mary   Bubbles came up and burst.
I wish I could have kept them.
They didn't seem important at the time.
I thought I was setting them free. But now I think they might have been messages and I didn't get them.
What do you think?

But **Gwen** *sits stunned, impassive.*

Mary *wrings out the hanky, puts it over her own face. Takes it off. Examines it.*

Mary   I can honestly say, if I'd known the trouble it would cause, I probably wouldn't have done it. But I wasn't thinking straight at the time. And I had to make a decision about who to save. Her or me. And I chose her.

It was clearer to me then than it is right now.
I better get this hanky dry.

Will you know me the next time?

Gwen *can't answer.*

Mary *starts to spin, round and round and round, waving the handkerchief in the wind. As she does so, the lights start to fade and music comes up: the sound of morris men dancing.*

End of Act One.

During the interval, **Alan** *erects the completed 'As Pants the Hart' well-dressing, sprays it with water to keep it fresh.*

Act Two

9

The church hall (now decked out with bunting). Whit-Monday.
Morris music drifts in from the Green outside where we can see
Gwen's well-dressing is mounted – 'As Pants the Hart'. It's
magnificent, a riot of colour.

Inside the hall, **Alan** *sweeps leftover flowerheads into mounds.* **Colin**
enters carrying a huge pile of tupperware containers.

Colin Help me out can you? I'm goin round in circles
lookin f'the cake stall.

Alan I don't know if she's set up yet.

Colin Well that explains a lot.

Colin *dumps the containers.*

Alan Gwen made all these?

Colin Yeah. She gets these spurts of energy. Look like you
could do with one.

Alan Stopped here last night, keep an eye on things.
Dressings at Etwall got vandalised quite bad last weekend.

Colin Y'kiddin?

Alan Nothing sacred these days. Gwen feeling better then,
if she managed all this?

Colin I think so.

Alan Quite humid in here yesterday. Praps that got to her.

Colin She was all-in last night when I got home, but then –

He indicates the cakes.

They're an endless source of mystery don't you find, women?

Alan No comment!

Colin   No. You've got the touch with them . . . Well mostly – sorry – I didn't mean anything . . .

Alan   You're all right.

Colin   No. My Gwen, hangs on your every word. Alan this Alan that.

Alan   Get off!

Colin   I'm serious. They're impressionable, see. Get these crazes. Fix on things. You'll find out.

Alan   Don't hold your breath.

Colin   I'm telling you!

Alan *picks up a box of flowerheads, goes towards the door.*

Alan   Oh – I'm glad you changed y'mind about the mirror.

Colin   Mirror? Oh – the thing! Damnblast it, I swear t'you I'll pick it up tomorrow.

Alan's *surprised.*

Alan   Gwen said you'd decided to get it done after all.

Colin   She what?

Alan   This morning, first thing.

Colin   Y'kiddin.

Alan   I'm not.

Gwen *enters.*

Gwen   Hi!

Colin   Hiya.

Audrey *comes in just behind her.*

Colin   Audrey.

Audrey   Colin.

Colin   Wasn't expectin t'see you this morning.

Gwen   Audrey was waiting when I got here first thing.

Audrey   Different clock still. I can't lie in.

Colin Right. (*to* **Gwen**) Listen, Alan was just saying you've changed your mind about the mirror.

Alan I'll er . . .

Alan *takes the box out.*

Gwen I was going t'mention it.

Colin When?

Gwen When I got chance.

Audrey I think it's a great idea.

Colin No . . . no . . . I was for gettin it done all along, it was Gwen draggin her heels.

Audrey Are these the cakes then?

Gwen Yeah.

Audrey *picks up some of the boxes.*

Colin I can bring those . . .

Audrey We can manage.

Audrey *heads for the door.* **Gwen** *starts to gather up the rest.* **Colin** *can hardly believe it.*

Colin Gwen?

He's obviously upset. **Gwen** *looks to* **Audrey**.

Gwen I'll catch you up.

Audrey I can wait.

Gwen Audrey . . . ?

Audrey Oh . . . sure.

Audrey *leaves.*

Colin Y'want t'get one of those stickers made.

Gwen What stickers?

Colin Y'know – 'my other life's a Porsche'.

Gwen *puts the boxes down.* **Alan** *appears at the door. Hangs back, waits unseen.*

Gwen   Why d'you do this, Colin?

Colin   What?

Gwen   No. Tell me. It's bad enough I've got her round my neck, without you. Everything I have that's to myself, you've got t'spoil it. Are y'jealous? Is that it?

Colin (*shouts*)   Gwen!

Beat.

I'm sorry, Gwen. You wear me out.

Gwen   No wonder I'm like I am.

Gwen *takes the cake boxes and heads out.*

Colin   And how's that? I can't keep up . . .

But she's gone now. **Colin** *breathes.* **Alan** *waits a beat, then enters.*

Alan   Off cake duty then?

Colin   Oh . . . Looks like it. I'll get on home, watch the match.

Alan   Who's playing?

Colin   It's er . . .

He falters.

I did know . . .

He's no idea. **Alan** *steps in.*

Alan   Only . . . I was hoping you might hang about.

Colin   Oh?

Alan   Just with being up all night I'm not exactly . . .

Colin   No, no. Course you're not. OK then.

Alan   Only if you fancy it, like . . .

Colin   Sure, yeah. I'm glad t'be useful.

Alan *smiles.*

Colin   Yeah.

Alan   Right, can y'get the other end o'that?

Colin   Sure.

They collapse the legs of a heavy trestle table.

Alan   Got it there?

Colin   Fine.

They lift it, carry it, prop it against the wall.

What next?

Alan   Grab a box, can you?

Colin *looks around, finds a cardboard box.* **Alan** *starts to sweep the hillocks of flowerheads, leaves and stems into one big pile.*

Alan   It's a bit close in here, but we'll soon be cleared away.

Colin   Wish I'd thought before I came down – could've picked up a fan from the office. Move the heat about a bit.

Alan   That'd be something.

Colin   I'll praps leave a decent interlude, then approach the Methodists with a quote for air-conditioning.

Alan   Why not!

Colin   Must hot up in here something chronic when it's full. Or are they meant t'suffer? Sorry – you're not . . . ?

Alan   God squad? No thanks.

Colin   Nor me. Well, not like this any road.

They set about filling the box.

Alan   Way I see it you've got one life, you go one way, and there's no coming back. Ought else is kidding y'self.

Colin   You see, you say that . . .

Alan   I do!

Colin   But . . .

Alan   But what . . . ?

Colin   Ah, nothing.

Alan   Go on.

Colin   It's just ... well ... every breath you and I take contains at least one atom of Julius Caesar's dying gasp.

Alan   Get off!

Colin   Might even be more than one, when y'think his dying breath was prob'ly a good big long one.

Alan   Are y'serious?

Colin   It's banking on a pretty good mix of his molecules with the rest of the earth's atmosphere. But after 2,000 years, I think that's fair enough.

Alan   I'd never thought about that before.

Colin   People don't.

Alan   No.

Colin   That might ... fit in somewhere ...

Mary *appears in the doorway.* **Alan** *sees her and she holds up the white flag of* **Colin**'s *hanky.*

Alan   Yeah. Yeah, it might.

Mary   For him.

Colin *nods to* **Alan**.

Colin   See you later.

Alan   Sure –

Alan *takes the box and leaves.* **Mary** *hands the hanky to* **Colin**.

Mary   I washed it.

Colin   Thank you. Y'didn't have to.

Mary   But it's special.

Colin   Ah. My initial. They're all like that.

Mary   You're lucky.

Colin   Am I?

Mary   Have someone do this for you.

Colin *reconsiders the hanky.*

Colin   She likes t'keep busy.

Mary   Has she said anything? About me?

Colin *shakes his head.*

Mary   I told her something. I don't know if she heard. Sorry I made him go away.

Colin   Like the weathermen, aren't you? One in, one out. We were only talkin.

Mary   What about?

Colin   Julius Caesar.

Mary   Oh.

Colin   You know about him?

Mary *shrugs.* **Colin** *declaims:*

Colin   'Infamy! Infamy! Everybody's got it in for me.'

Mary *is blank.*

Colin   He got stabbed on the steps.

Mary   Oh.

Colin   I was just saying how there's molecules of his last breath all through the atmosphere. You've probably just breathed one in.

Mary   Now?

Colin   Almost certainly.

Mary *is put out.*

Colin   What's up?

Mary   I don't want Julius Caesar in me.

Colin   It's not just him. It's everyone . . . Everyone who ever breathed. Ever lived.

Mary   Wait.

Mary *suddenly strains to think, almost grasps something.*

Colin   Listen . . .

Mary   No, wait!

She struggles to pursue the idea.

Colin   Look it's only a bit of fun . . .

Mary   What?

Colin   Fun.

Mary   Bye.

She waves, rushes off, leaving **Colin** *alone with his hanky.*

Colin   Fun.

10

The landing stage. **Mary** *breathes desperately, huge great gasps in and out, working herself into a terrible state. After a while, she sinks to her knees, continues panting, slumps to the ground, gasping for breath.*

Alan *enters, rushes over, calls out, panicking.*

Alan   Colin! Colin!

Alan *kneels down, cradles* **Mary** *awkwardly .*

Alan (*to* **Mary**)   You're all right, you're all right.

Mary *continues to gasp. He calls out again:*

Alan   Somebody . . . ! You're all right . . . you're all right . . . I can't do this . . .

Audrey *arrives, running.*

Audrey   What happened?

Alan   I can't do this . . .

Audrey   Make sure she doesn't swallow her tongue . . .

Alan   You're all right . . .

Colin *arrives.*

Colin   What's . . . ?

He eases **Alan** *out of the way and takes over.*

What's happened, Alan?

Alan   She was . . . breathing – hard – like panting – then she fell down . . .

Colin   Overbreathing...

He manoeuvres **Mary** *into the recovery position.*

I need a bag or something. Have you got anything?

Obviously not. **Colin** *searches his pocket, finds the hanky. He places the hanky over* **Mary**'*s face, covering her nose and mouth.* **Gwen** *arrives.*

Gwen   What happened?

Colin   It's all right, Gwen, don't flap.

(*to* **Mary**)   Just try and breathe steady for me now, breathe steady . . . y'silly thing, what were y'thinkin of? Breathe steady, pet. OK now . . .

Mary'*s breathing slows a bit.*

Alan   She was like panting, on purpose.

Gwen   Messing about.

Colin   It's my fault. Something I told her.

Gwen   What?

Mary *fights to sit up.*

Colin (*to* **Mary**)   No, love.

She settles a little.

Just something stupid. God, I'm stupid. Can you see if there's any St John's Ambulance or anything.

Alan   You'll stay with her?

Colin   Course.

Alan *rushes off.* **Mary** *pushes the hanky from her face.*

Colin   You're all right, love, just breathe steady for me.

Gwen   She's all right, she's just overheated.

Audrey   Get her a drink, Gwen. I'll wait . . .

Gwen   Well I'll try.

Gwen *leaves.* **Mary** *tries to get up but* **Audrey** *intervenes.*

Audrey   Oh no.

Mary I'm all right.

Colin What were y'thinkin of?

Mary *fights to her feet.*

Mary I've got to go.

Audrey Not by yourself.

Audrey *puts an arm round* **Mary**. **Mary** *pushes her off, angry.*

Mary Get off me.

Audrey *pulls back.*

Mary Leave me alone.

Mary *makes her way off, along the riverbank.* **Audrey** *is about to follow.*

Audrey Shouldn't we . . . ?

Colin No point.

Audrey *gives up on the idea.*

Colin Sod it all. Sod my big bloody mouth.

Beat.

Audrey I'll see what's happened t'Gwen.

Colin Look – Audrey – I'm sorry. About earlier. I know you've got a lot on. It must be hard.

Audrey *nods. A moment of unexpected sympathy, interrupted when* **Gwen** *arrives with a cup of water.*

Audrey Too late.

Gwen What did I tell you!

Audrey *turns back to* **Colin**.

Audrey It's not as hard as you think. Sooner or later you ask yourself. Am I going to spend the rest of my life with the wrong person? Once you've got an answer to that, the decision makes itself.

Beat.

Gwen We should get back, Audrey.

Colin   I wouldn't want you to miss anything.

Gwen   They've got hot dogs going.

Colin   Smashing.

The three stand in a deadlock until **Colin** *breaks away, goes to sit down on the landing stage, flicks bits of stone into the water.*

Gwen   Audrey, can y'just be a bit more careful what you say to Colin?

Audrey   Have you told him?

Gwen   Told him what?

Audrey   I thought you'd maybe said something –

Gwen   No...!

Audrey   I feel awkward with him. Sorry for him. I think you should say something. Go on, Gwen.

Gwen   Not now!

Audrey   Well then when...?

Gwen   Anyway, what would I say? What is there to say? You want too much.

Audrey   I want to be with you.

Gwen   You don't leave anything for me to want.

Audrey   Why don't you tell him?

Gwen   Listen, Audrey, you've come at a bad time. I didn't like t'say so before, I was pleased t'see you...

Audrey   Pleased to...?

Gwen   Maybe another time things would be different...

Audrey   When?

Gwen   Another time.

Audrey   You wrote t'me!

Gwen   Not asking you t'come. Leave your husband, lock, stock and barrel... I'm shocked by it, Audrey.

Audrey   Don't do this, Gwen.

Gwen   You should go back and think it over.

Audrey   I've nothing to go back to . . .

Gwen   I can't help that. You're too much! Every time I turn round you're there. No good'll come of it, Audrey. I sometimes wonder if I didn't marry Colin just t'get you off my back.

Audrey   No . . .

Gwen   You cling so . . . Like a bit of chewing gum on my shoe – I want t'scrape you off me.

Audrey   When you didn't want me, I went away. And I would have stayed, but you wrote to me. You started it up again.

Gwen   Started what up? I did no such thing.

Audrey   You can't just send me away again, Gwen . . .

Gwen   I can.

Audrey   You want me, Gwen.

Gwen   I want to cover my face when you come near. I want to block my nose, understand? Now get away. Go on . . .

Gwen *storms off.*

Audrey   Gwen . . . ? I've nowhere to go!

Audrey *pursues her.*

11

The landing stage, later. **Alan** *arrives with two plastic pint glasses filled with beer.*

Alan   Mary went.

Colin   Yeah.

Alan   Gwen told me.

He hands **Colin** *a pint.*

How d'you know what t'do?

Colin   I'm the First Aid at work. Plus I've spent that many Saturday nights in watchin *Casualty*, I could have me own adenoids out with a rear view mirror and a crochet hook.

Alan   Good thing. Cheers.

They drink.

You've no kids of your own?

Colin   No, we can't. Couldn't. Gwen's got something missing. So.

Who is she?

Alan *thinks and drinks.*

Alan   He used t'move the hands on the clock at work. Move 'em forward t'get off early'n'see her. She used t'sit across the road, on the street sign, swinging her legs. He couldn't wait. So full of . . . I don't know . . . life. Sounds daft.

Colin   No.

Alan   Seventeen.

Colin *sucks in breath.*

Alan   I let him have the delivery van weekends. I knew what he mostly got up to in it. Monday mornings I could smell her in there.

They had this big set-to one Friday night. She finished with him. He drove down here, Steven.

We had these ropes in the back of the van always, y'know for hauling.

Tied his legs t'the steering wheel.

Knots I'd taught him.

Put his foot down.

His hand traces the van's flight off the landing stage, into the river and down.

I got the call round midnight. There was no sign he tried t'undo the ropes.

Oh Christ . . . I don't want any harm t'come to her. I'm past that. I just want to forget.

They sit in silence for a while. **Colin** *seems about to speak, changes his mind. Then forces himself.*

Colin   I'm a plumber. I know about water and air and fire. And I know energy can't be destroyed. It has to go somewhere. Pass into something else – anything else more or less. Just some things're better at soaking it up than others.

Alan   I know you're right. I know all these things're true. But I can't make anything useful out of 'em.

Colin   My dad died last year. Blessing in some ways, he'd gone senile, d'you see? Getting worse by the day.

It's a terrible way t'go. We had t'put him in hospital t'be looked after. Got even more confused then. Always looking f'things from his old house at first. Then he seemed to forget that too. Forgot everything. In the end I don't think he'd any idea who I was. He was pleased enough t'see me like, but only as a friendly face.

But the last time I saw him he spoke to me in a way I could understand f'the first time in ages. He'd been just gibbering for months, but this day he looked at the wall ahead of him – big blank hospital wall and said clear as clear: 'Well will you look at that? All the years we've lived here and I never knew there was a door there . . . ' And I looked, but there was nothing. 'Right there,' he said. 'All these years.'

I don't know what it means.
I don't know what he could really see.
But I understood. Something.

Never told anyone before.

Alan   You're a good man, Colin.

Colin   Get on!

He gets up.

Y'want t'get some sleep. All look better in the morning.

Alan   Y'reckon?

Colin F'sure.

Alan *gets up too.*

Alan Drop by in the week, maybe . . .

Colin Yeah. I'd like that.

Alan Not comin now?

Colin I'm in no hurry.

Alan *nods, understands. Leaves* **Colin** *stargazing. After a while,* **Colin** *opens his arms to embrace the night sky.*

At the landing stage, **Audrey** *arrives lost, tired. Sees* **Colin**, *considers leaving, then decides to stay.*

Audrey I can go . . .

Colin *turns, surprised.* **Audrey** *looks defeated.*

Colin No. Stay . . . if you want.

Audrey *comes down onto the landing stage.*

Colin Used t'play down here when you were kids.

Audrey Yeah.

Colin She told me. Bit different then.

Audrey *looks over to the other bank.*

Audrey All that was allotments.

Colin My uncle had one.

Audrey And Gwen's dad. Didn't grow much.

Colin No?

Audrey Just a place t'get away to I suppose.
Did you go there sometimes?

Colin Sometimes.

Audrey We did.

Colin Never noticed you. I'd be more interested in snails then.

Audrey I remember a man grew fruit. Raspberries, gooseberries. The birds used t'take them. He caught this bird in a net one time. Hung it upside down by its feet – alive still – t'scare off the others. Horrible.

Colin   Yeah.

Audrey   Gwen's dad said it was dead the next day. Wore itself out. Twisting and turning.

Beat.

Colin   Gwen not around?

Audrey   I think she's gone home. I looked everywhere else.

Colin   You've got a lot on.

Audrey   I've got nothing on. Not a thing.

Colin   Had a fall-out?

Audrey *nods.*

Colin   She's a bit prickly at the moment.

Audrey   She thinks I should go back.

Colin   She can be unkind.

Beat.

Audrey   I love her anyway.

Colin   I know.

Audrey   I can't help it.

Colin   I know that too.

Beat.

There's no chance of you and Philip mebbe . . .

Audrey   No. He's a nice man, Philip. But I never . . . you know.

Colin   I see.

Audrey   Not like you and Gwen.

Colin   Oh, no. Head over heels we were. I was.

Audrey *doesn't reassure.*

Colin   It was a good do. We had dancing. I remember saying t'Gwen, aren't I supposed t'dance with the bridesmaid? But you'd already gone.

Audrey   Not much fun dancing on your own.

Colin   I'm so sorry. I didn't think.
I've not danced in years. Probably can't any more.

Audrey   I bet you can.

Colin   It's clear enough in m'mind, but I doubt m'bones can follow.

He turns away from her, upset.

God, I'm sorry . . .

The two of them stay like this for a while, **Colin** *hiding his face. Then* **Audrey** *approaches him from behind. She gently puts her arms around him. Holds him, her face resting against his shoulders, both of them lost.*

Suddenly **Colin** *turns and hugs her for a long time, then kisses her very gently on the lips.*

Audrey   Colin . . .

Colin   I've got you. I've got you now . . .

He kisses her again with increasing passion.

Colin   You're all right.

Audrey *responds.*

Colin   You're all right.

At the Green, **Gwen** *enters. She approaches the well-dressing, takes it in. Then she steps closer, as close as she can. She reaches out and digs her fingers into the soft clay round the eyes of the hart. She digs it out, throws the clay to the ground, competely unaware of* **Colin** *and* **Audrey** *in their passionate embrace.*

12

Alan's *shop, a couple of weeks later / The landing stage.*

Alan *pulls the upholstery from* **Gwen**'s *headboard. The bell sounds and* **Mary** *stands in the doorway, nervous but full of new resolve.*

Mary   I came to say thank you. I know you helped me.

Alan *scarcely breathes.* **Mary** *eases herself in.*

Mary   I would have come sooner. But it took time.

She looks around the room.

Not changed.

Alan   Don't push your luck.

Mary   No.

She looks at the photo of **Steven**.

Can I stay? For a minute.

Alan *doesn't say 'no'.* **Mary** *runs her hands over the back of the swivel chair. Takes in the feel of it. Finally sits down.*

Mary   That picture's so sad, it makes you forget the things not in it . . .

Alan *can't move.* **Mary** *sits out the silence. She's not going anywhere. Not this time.*

At the landing stage, by the river, **Colin** *lies on top of* **Audrey**, *kisses her, breaks away.*

Colin   I'm afraid. I'm scared I'll cross some line with you and I won't be able t'go back.

Audrey   Then stop.

Colin   What if it's too late? What if it's already happened? I can't keep up with my heart. It's like a hat that's blown away and I can't catch it back. I've always almost got it, then a gust comes from nowhere and it's off . . . I need this.

Audrey   Then take it.

She nods, **Colin** *pulls off his shirt.*

Take it.

She reaches up for him, pulls him down onto her.

*In **Alan**'s shop, **Mary** and **Alan** as before. Suddenly **Alan** speaks.*

Alan   We weren't allowed t'see the body, y'know. It was so blown up with water. Swollen.

Mary   I know.

Alan   That van. It had our name on the side. Bradley. My name.

Mary   So what're you saying – it was bad for trade?

Alan *snaps –*

Alan   You watch your mouth I'll put you through the middle of next week you won't know what has hit you!

Mary *doesn't flinch.*

Mary   This picture.

Alan   What about it?

Mary   I was outside, watching the day you took it. Steven watching the clock. Because he used t'move the hands t'get out faster.

Alan   Cos you used t'come early t'meet him. Y'knew he didn't finish till half past. But y'had t'come early, drive him half mad.

Mary   And why did I do that?

Alan   Y'couldn't help it.

Mary   Watching the two of you work. Starlings gather on telephone wires. Sky all pinky. I'd bunk off lessons, lie through my teeth, go to all that trouble t'get here early so I could just watch . . . and he'd always cut it short. Always. And you let him.

Alan   Course I did.

Mary   Why?

Alan   Y'should've seen the state he was in.

Mary   Were y'jealous?

Alan   What?

Mary   The way y'used t'wave us off sometimes.

Alan   No...

Mary   I wouldn't have missed it for anything. When you stood at the door...

She raises her hand in a parting wave.

'Have fun...'

Alan   So what?

Mary   The way you looked at me.

Alan   What way?
I never looked at you any way...

Mary   I think y'did.

Alan   What is this?

Mary   Y'know it!

Alan   You're sick.

Mary   Don't tell me y'never thought about it.

Alan   I didn't.

Mary   Liar! People don't look at other people like that! You can't look at someone like that without thinking about it!

Alan   There's a difference between thinking and doing.

Mary   Why is there?

Alan   Cos otherwise we'd all be like you.

Mary   Would that be so bad?

Alan   You've no shame.

Mary   I've no hope.

Alan   And what hope I had you've seen to. 'Bradley and Son.' That's what the sign says. Well you put paid t'that.

Mary   He wasn't your son.

Alan   No, he was more than that . . . he was my only . . . *only*.

Mary   I know.

Alan   Y'don't know! Y'don't know a thing. I'm a sad fuck, me, y'know. I work here in this dark dank friggin place . . . and what gets me through is . . . is . . . I wonder: will someone some day turn up a piece that I made? Mm . . . ? Will they say . . . 'look – his hands were here, and here, and here . . .', lay their hands on top . . . feel something . . . some bloody thing of how it was . . . of how I was . . . ?

But they won't! They'll paint it green. Throw it on the fire one night and I'll be gone . . .

Mary   I do know.

Alan   How can you say that after what you did? Why didn't y'tell him you were expecting the baby?

Mary   I'd never've been rid of him. It wasn't any good between us.

Alan   So you killed him?

Mary   I kept him short all the time. Pushing him away. But he couldn't get enough of it.

Alan   Y'couldn't just finish it, let him find someone else.

Mary   I tried! He didn't want anyone else. Don't you see? Even knowing . . .

Look. I didn't love him. I feel bad enough about that. But I didn't kill him.

Alan   So who did?

Mary   We should stop this . . .

Alan   Who killed him? You tell me.

Mary *runs her hands along the desktop. Feels the wood warm on her skin.*

Mary   Let me stay here a bit. Where I can see you. Don't make it all have been for nothing.

13

Gwen *and* **Colin**'*s, months later.* **Colin** *stands shirtless, his arms around someone.*

Colin   In the middle there's nothing, I'm just numb. But round the edge – I'm life – I'm all sensation.

The woman – **Gwen** *– wriggles free.*

Gwen   There's no time.

Colin   No – Gwen.

He catches her back, hugs her, hard. There's an undertone of violence in his desperation.

Colin   Gwen.

Gwen   What?

Colin   You know what . . .

Gwen   No.

Colin   Yes . . .

Gwen   I don't want to . . .

Colin   Gwen, please . . .

Gwen   No, it hurts . . .

Colin   We'll be careful . . .

Gwen   I'm too dry.

She shoves him away from her.

Satisfied?

He pulls her back, clings to her, softer now.

Colin   Gwen, come with me. I need you . . .

She pulls away from him.

Gwen   I should've known. That's what all this is about.

Colin   Please.

Gwen   How many times?

She picks up a shirt.

Are you taking this shirt?

Colin   I haven't thought.

Gwen   Well, you better think if you want that button sewn back.

Colin   Why won't you talk to me, Gwen?

Gwen   I won't have Audrey here and the place look a mess.

Colin   Audrey?

Gwen   She's calling for a drink before you go.

Colin   Since when?

Gwen   I asked her.

Colin   Why?

Gwen   Why not? She's always wanting t'see me . . .

Colin   She calls you?

Gwen   And I don't want t'see her on her own.

Colin   How often?

Gwen   This is the last opportunity while you're here.

Colin   So you thought you'd make use of me?
I'm about t'go off for a fortnight.

Gwen   A week.

Colin   Nine days.

Gwen   Eight days and a couple of hours, Colin, you're being silly.

Colin *hurls a last few things into his case.*

Colin   Your own husband and you're terrified t'spend two minutes by yourself with me. Y'best friend, y'can't stand t'see on her own.

Gwen   You don't know what she's like.

Colin   What if I did, Gwen?

Gwen   You don't.

Colin   What if you're wrong about that? Tell me something I don't know about Audrey, Gwen. Mmm? I challenge you to tell me something I don't know!

Gwen   When she touches me . . . I . . . I feel like I've got no skin!

Colin *is taken aback.*

Colin   Gwen?

Gwen   No!

Colin   Gwen . . . ? Look at me, Gwen. Look at me! What d'you see? Anything y'want? Or recognise? Or wonder about?

She finally looks at him.

Colin   No. I'm sorry. You're a dead-end, Gwen.

Gwen   Don't say that . . .

Colin   You've no use for anything I've got t'give you.

He picks up his case.

Gwen   Where are you going?

Colin   What choice have you given me?

Colin *takes the case and leaves.*

Gwen   Colin . . . Colin!

Audrey *enters, catching* **Gwen** *off-balance.*

Audrey   No Colin?

Gwen   No . . . airport. You've t'check in ages ahead.

Audrey   I'm surprised you're not going with him.

Gwen   Well I'm not.

Audrey   I thought you might. Get some sun, now the weather's turned.

Gwen   I'm not much of a one for sun.

Audrey   And you'll miss him.

Gwen   Glad t'have him out from under my feet.

Audrey   But not glad enough t'leave him.

Gwen   No.

Audrey   What if he left you?

Gwen   Oh, give it up, Audrey...

Audrey   You said before he'd nowhere to go. What if he found somewhere?

Gwen   He wouldn't...

Audrey   How can you be sure?

Gwen   He's my husband! I would know!

Audrey   And what am I?

Gwen   I don't know.

Audrey   You should never have led me to hope.

Gwen   You didn't need much encouragement!

Audrey   You were going to leave him!

Gwen   And then what?

Audrey   Why did you do it, Gwen? Bring me back here? Just to see if you still could?

Gwen   This is a difficult time, Audrey...

Audrey   It'll never happen, will it?

Gwen   That's not what I said...

Audrey   Say it, Gwen! Say 'never'! There is such a thing. It goes back to back with 'always'.

Gwen   No...

Audrey   Say 'never', Gwen. Learn t'say it before it's too late.

Gwen   Y'talk about the past as though it was yesterday. A lot's happened since then.

Audrey   There's been nothing!

Gwen   Colin's not nothing!

Audrey   No. He's not.

Gwen   At night, Audrey, I hold on to that man, I hold on so tight because I'm afraid that if I don't I might blow clean away. I used t'read those letters you sent and let my mind wander ... but it got harder and harder t'bring it back in.

Audrey   Then why don't you go with him to Italy?

Gwen   It's no business of yours! Why d'you have t'have everything of mine! It's not my fault your life's like it is. I didn't make you marry Philip. I didn't make your mother die. I don't want the responsibility any more.

Audrey   Why don't you go, Gwen!

Gwen   Y'know, I've imagined a world where you were dead – and it was terrible, but I'd give anything to imagine a world where you'd never been born. What would I be like then?

Audrey   Gwen ... ?

Gwen   I once said to my mother 'I wish Audrey had never been born.'

Audrey   When did you ... ?

Gwen   And she told me that was a terrible thing to say. She told me all about you ...

Audrey   Told you what ... ?

Gwen   There were scars on the placenta when you were born. Actual scars where your mother almost lost you, but you held on, clung on you were so strong.

Audrey   That's not true ...

Gwen   And you're still the same.

Audrey   I'm nothing like that ...

Gwen   What would I have been like not afraid? With Colin – we'd make love, and after ... after ... I'd go and wash myself out. I'd wash him out of me, because I was afraid.

Audrey   No ...

Gwen   Of you!
Well I'm cutting you off now. I don't want you! Why can't
you understand, I want Colin?

Audrey   Colin's gone.

Gwen   He'll come back . . .

Audrey   Colin's gone, Gwen!

Gwen   I want Colin. I'm frightened without him. I want to
tell him what I've done!

Beat.

Audrey   Then you better go and get him.

Gwen   I can't.

Audrey   You know where he is.

Gwen   And he knows where I am.

Audrey   You really think he's coming back?

Gwen *entertains the possibility that he might not.*

Gwen   If I'm sorry enough . . . if I'm sorry enough he'll
come back.

Audrey *leaves.*

14

Mary *and* **Alan** *sit in the darkened shop as before. They've been there
for a long long long long time.* **Mary** *examines her chair.*

Mary   Steven fixed this when it got broke.

Alan *nods.*

Mary   His great-grandad made it. Lasted hundred years.

Alan *looks away.*

Mary   Longer'an any of us will.

After a while:

Adam and Eve and Pinch-Me
Went down t'the river t'bathe.
Adam and Eve were drowned.
Who d'you think was saved?

He looks up at her.

Who d'you think?

Alan *holds out his hand.*

Alan   Pinch me.

Mary *shakes her head.*

Alan   Pinch me.

But she doesn't. **Alan**'s *insistent now.*

Alan   Pinch me!

Mary   I wouldn't hurt you for the world.

Alan *starts to cry.* **Mary** *rushes to him, takes his face in her hands.*

Mary   Oh no, oh no ... Kiss away your tears ...

She does so.

... make you better or send you blind.

She wraps her arms around him, holds him as he sobs.

15

Gwen *and* **Colin**'s.

Gwen *alone in the early evening.*

Gwen   It's time y'had some new hankies, Col. I'm going
t'get some new and embroider them for you. You'll like that,
won't you? Yes. I think you will. And do something with
these sheets. They're so worn. Turn the sides to the middle.
No one need know. We've made do, now I'll mend.

She shakes out **Colin**'s *shirt. Puts her arms around it as if he were in it, wraps the sleeves around her shoulders. She buries her face in it. Smells something. Smells the shirt again, and again.*

No . . . ?

She flattens the shirt out, studies it. It can't be true.

16

The beach at Ostia/ The landing stage.

Audrey *lies in her bikini, shiny with sun oil.* **Colin** *sweats it out in his swimming trunks.* **Audrey** *reads a trashy paperback.* **Colin** *is bored.*

Colin   It's hot.

Audrey *looks up for a moment, then back.* **Colin** *waits.*

Colin   Sand gets everywhere.

No reaction.

I don't want to go back.

Audrey   People always feel like that on holiday.

Colin   Some people can't wait to get back. People who've got something to go back to.

Audrey   People who can't relax.

Colin   I can't relax but I don't want to go back.
Audrey . . . ?

Audrey *(firmly)*   No.

Colin   Why not?

Audrey   You don't mean it.

Colin   What if I did?

Audrey   You don't.

Colin   I could.

Audrey   Gwen.

Beat.

Colin   I bought her a postcard. What will I write?

Audrey   It'll get there after you do anyway.

Colin   Don't say that.

She goes back to her book.

Heat doesn't bother you.

Audrey   Less to think about.

Colin   That's the holiday not the heat.

Audrey *continues to read.* **Colin** *leans over and strokes her.*

Colin   Stripes on your tummy. Like a tiger.

Audrey *rolls away.*

Audrey   Stretch marks. Write your postcard.

Colin   I can't.

Audrey *gives up reading.*

Audrey   I might go for a swim.

Colin   Looks dirty.

Audrey   D'you think?

Colin   Says in the brochure the current's 'deceptive'.

Audrey   I've swum in places like this before. Never drowned yet.

Colin   You wouldn't drown here.

Audrey   No?

Colin   I'd rescue you. Pull you back to dry land.

Beat.

Audrey *reaches out, touches* **Colin** *gently.*

I'd give you the kiss of life, Audrey. Breathe my breath into you. In, out, in, out . . . You'd be born again. A fresh start.

They sit like this for a while.

Audrey   Write your postcard, Colin.

She hardens herself, withdraws her hand.

Come on! 'Dear Gwen, the beach in this little cove is clean and deserted. In the day, the sky is a dazzling turquoise, at night it's a canopy punctured by stars. I wish I could be seeing them with you. I wish we could be sitting here together drinking our cocktails and listening to waves lap, lap lap at the golden shore. Some things you could not find out from a brochure.'

Colin   If I turn over will you oil my back?

Colin *turns away.*

Audrey   You've got to go back, Colin.

Colin   Can you make it the sunblock? It's m'first time on m'front.

Audrey *fishes for the bottle of lotion, puts some on her finger.*

Audrey   You have got to go back.

She starts to paint definite letters onto his back.

Colin   Mmm...

Audrey   Nice?

Colin   Yeah.

Audrey   Gwen needs you.

Colin   What about what I need?

Audrey   What you never had you never miss.

Colin   I've had what I need. I've got it now.

Audrey   No, you've not.

Colin   Yes...

Audrey   Shsh.

She continues gently painting the letters in the white lotion.

Shshsh... Have a sleep now... It'll seem simpler after a sleep.

Colin *drifts off in the heat. Audrey looks up at the sun beating down on* **Colin**'s *back.*

Lights come up on the landing stage. It is evening. **Gwen** *holds up* **Audrey**'s *penny.*

Gwen   Have it.

She throws it back into the river.

Have your stupid wish.

17

Alan *works in the shop.* **Gwen** *enters, anxious, high energy.*

Alan   Hi! I was going t'call you today, 'bout the mirror. It's come up lovely. I've got it out the back.

Gwen   Oh, I was actually looking for Mary.
(*Calls out.*) Mary!!!
Is she here?

Alan   Right . . . just a mo – MARY?

Mary (*offstage*)   I'm coming!

Alan   So's Christmas. Get a shuffle on. Colin's back soon, in't he?

Gwen   Sunday, yes.

Alan   Hallowe'en!

Mary *enters, looks pissed off. Brightens when she sees* **Gwen**.

Mary   Hiya!

Alan   What's the long face for?

Mary   Splinter.

Alan   Let's see?

She shows him.

That's nothing. Soon work its way out.

Mary   I thought they went through y'blood and then stuck in y'heart.

Alan   If that were true I'd have a heart like a hedgehog.
Give it here.

He squeezes it a bit, then sucks it.

You've made a right mess. What have you been doing it with?

Mary   Needle.

Gwen   Why doesn't Alan fetch me the mirror so I can have
a look at it?

Mary   Yeah – It's fantastic what he's done with it.

Alan   OK. I'll get some Germolene while I'm at it.

He leaves the women alone. **Gwen** *is peculiarly aggressive.*

Gwen   I looked for you at the park but you weren't there.

Mary   No...

Gwen   What are you doing here?

Mary   Helping out.

Gwen   You and him like dit and twit!

Mary   We're... OK. Yeah.

Gwen   Turn up for the books.

Mary   It's more than I hoped for.

Gwen *shouts.*

Gwen   Don't come the butter wouldn't melt with me!
What you told me that day. Is it true?

Mary   Look, I wasn't the full ticket when I told you...

Gwen   Was it true?

Mary   Well...

Gwen   Was it...?

Mary   Yeah.

Gwen   Y'killed your baby.

Mary   Yes.

Gwen   Just like that?

Mary   No...

Gwen   Why aren't you in prison?

Mary   I went to hospital.

Gwen   Murderers go to prison.

Mary   It's called infanticide, it's different.

Gwen   You take a life, that's murder.

Mary   No, it's different, that's why they have a special law...

Gwen   You murdered that child!

Mary   If I'd aborted her no one would have cared. That's what they wanted me t'do. In a hospital. With strangers.

Gwen   That doesn't give you the right to kill her.

Mary   She was mine, part of me. When I looked in the water, the only face I could see was mine.
She didn't struggle... She was part of me! That can't be murder!

Gwen   What was her name?

Mary   She was only a week.

Gwen   What did you call her?

Mary   Nothing...

Gwen   You must have called her something.

Mary   Not a name.

Gwen   But...

Mary *remembers. She's horrified as it sinks in.*

Mary   Love. I called her love. I didn't mean to. I didn't mean to call her anything, it just happened...

Gwen   You wicked girl.

Mary   Why did I do that...?

Gwen   You wicked wicked terrible girl...

Mary *covers her head as* **Gwen** *slaps at her over and over.*

Mary   Why did I give her a name . . . ?

Alan *returns, carrying the packaged mirror.*

Alan   What the . . . get off her . . . GET OFF!

He pushes **Gwen** *away, tries to comfort* **Mary**.

Mary   It was murder!

Alan   No.

Gwen   Yes!

Mary   Yes, yes. She's right.

Alan (*to* **Gwen**)   What are you doing?

Mary *breaks away into the back of the shop.*

Gwen   She should have been punished!

Alan   Here, take your damn mirror.

Gwen   I don't want it any more.

Alan   Well that's two of us.

He shoves the mirror over to **Gwen**, *opens the door wide.*

Go on. Take it and get out.

Gwen   I can't . . .

Alan   Go!

Gwen *starts to haul the huge package out of the shop.* **Alan** *slams the door behind her. Locks it.*

Alan   Mary . . . Mary?

Eventually **Mary** *reappears.*

Mary   I'm right at home here with all these broken things. Can you repair me, can you?

18

Audrey *sits at a table in a bar in Ostia, a campari and soda before her. She has a deck of cards, is playing 'Patience'.* **Colin** *enters.*

Colin   D'you want a . . .

She nods to her drink.

Fine.

He hesitates.

I don't know whether to or not.

She continues with the cards.

No, I won't. We're not staying long anyway are we? No.

He sits down.

All sorted out. It was the one speaks English on the desk.

Audrey   They all speak English.

Colin   Well, better English, then. It'll be on a tray, t'have in the room. They don't open the breakfast room till seven thirty.

Audrey   Too late.

Colin   I explained. D'you want t'drink up then?

Audrey   In a minute.

Colin   D'you want to stay?

Audrey   I don't mind.

Colin   Only I'll get a drink if you do.

Audrey   Whatever.

Colin   I say let's go. It's the last night. We want to enjoy it.

Audrey   I am.

Colin   Together.

Audrey *picks up her glass, takes a drink.*

Audrey   All right?

Colin   I'm not trying t'hurry you. I just want t'know.

Audrey   What?

Colin   If I should get a drink.

Audrey   I've said, it's up to you.

Colin   I'll get one.

He stands up, digs in his pockets. He takes out a roll of notes and a handful of change.

Got any coins? I don't want t'break into a big note and get stuck with the change.

She checks her purse, gives him a couple of coins.

Audrey   That's it.

Colin   Not enough, I won't bother.

Audrey   Have one if you want one.

Colin   I don't know. You can't change coins back into English. I don't like finding old foreign money in the backs of drawers. Horrible smelling and worth nothing.

Audrey   You're bound to need money at the airport anyway.

Colin   That's true.

He sits down again.

I'll think about it.

Audrey *sips her drink, largely for* **Colin**'s *benefit. They sit in silence until* **Colin** *can bear it no longer.*

Colin   Have you enjoyed it then? I mean is it so bad for me to ask? Is it? I don't know. I don't know what I've done wrong.

Audrey   I don't know what you want me to say.

Colin   I want you.

Audrey   I know that.

Colin   No – that's what I want you t'say. Give me a clue, Audrey, I'm so far out of my depth . . .

Audrey   I'm not coming back.

Colin   What?

Audrey   I'll stay here a while. Then go on somewhere else.

Colin   Where?

Audrey   I'll see.

Colin   What about me?

Audrey   You'll survive.

Colin   I don't want t'just survive . . .

But **Audrey** *is plainly determined.*

What shall I tell Gwen?

Audrey   Whatever you like.

Colin   She'll want t'know what's happened to you.

Audrey   I can't think why.

Colin   Because she cares about you, Audrey. Praps more than you might think. She might just worry about whether you're dead or alive.

Audrey *turns over more cards.*

Audrey   Alive. Tell her I'm alive.

19

Gwen *sits by the still-wrapped mirror. She holds a postcard. Reads:*

Gwen   'Commercial and overcrowded though the hotel's nice. You can't swim cos the sea's too polluted so I'm further down the coast. Went to Ostia Antica where sand preserved ruins. Saw how Romans lived second century AD. House with mosaic like a well-dressing: Castor and Pollux, twins born to Leda after raped by Zeus disguised as swan. Can't be sure which of these people were real. It's too long ago. Colin.'

She turns to the mirror. Takes up a pair of scissors. Finds the string. Snip, snip, snip. She gently tears away the wrapping paper. Pulls some of it away, revealing part of the mirror. Looks in.

20

The end of the day. **Alan** *stands on a chair, turns the shop clock back by an hour.* **Mary** *finishes clearing up, covers pieces with white dust sheets. She pulls one of the sheets over her head, makes a strange howling sound, waves her arms. A child's idea of a ghost.* **Alan** *looks round.*

Mary   Are you scared?

Alan   Nearly peed my pants.

Mary *sits in the swivel chair – the Steven chair – spins round and round and round, completely covered by the sheet.* **Alan** *watches for a moment, then climbs down, stops the chair. He touches* **Mary**'*s face through the sheet. Strokes it lightly. Finds the mouth. Gently kisses it.* **Mary** *scarcely returns the kiss though she shows no sign of resistance.* **Alan** *traces her features through the fabric again, then lifts the sheet to reveal the face. Stays close.*

Alan   Listen, Mary . . .

Mary   Yeah.

Alan   I'm not really . . . Girls – f'me – they're not really the thing.

Mary   I know that.

Alan   Do you?

Mary *nods.*

Beat.

Alan   You're full of surprises, you.

I shouldn't let you stay. It's a gloomy sort of place, this. Wasted all my sunny days here.

I should make you go away, somewhere better.

Shall I?

Mary   No. We'll stay here together, you and me. In the darkness, but not touching.

Like apples in a drawer, getting ripe.

21

Colin *is home. He throws his jacket down over his case.*

Gwen   It was a lovely postcard.

Colin   Can't believe it got here so fast.

Gwen   No, it's unusual. Colin . . . ?

She approaches, puts her arms round him. **Colin** *winces, pushes her away.*

Colin   Sorry. I got burnt.

Gwen   Oh dear. Shall I look?

Colin   It's all right.

Gwen   Let me. Please.

Colin *gives in. She helps him off with his shirt. Against the red background of his sunburnt back are words spelled out in white, written in sunblock.* **Gwen** *reads them.*

Audrey *sits in her hotel room in Ostia.*

Audrey   'I don't love you any more.'

Gwen *is silent.*

Colin   Is it bad?

Gwen   Yes it is quite bad.

Colin   Let me see in the mirror.

Gwen   No. There's no need. I'll put something on it.

Colin   You don't have to.

Gwen   I'd like to.

Colin *acquiesces.* **Gwen** *works cream into the burn. After a while:*

Gwen   Audrey's been away for a bit.

Colin   Has she?

Gwen   Don't know if she's back yet.

Colin   She's maybe not coming back.

Gwen   D'you think she might not?

Colin   I think there's a chance.

Gwen   Y'never know with Audrey. Like a bad penny.

Colin   I think she won't.

Beat.

Gwen   And what will she do?

Colin   She'll start again.

Gwen   On her own?

Colin   Back at the beginning, on her own.

Gwen   This is the one I mended.

She slips a fresh shirt onto **Colin**.

I expect there's more t'mend in y'case.

Colin   I expect.

*He goes to look out of the landing window at the misty autumn evening.
He stretches, his arms raised high and tense, then falling slowly,
controlled, like wings meeting resistance.*

I've got so much t'give.

Gwen   And you've got me.

Colin   Yes.

Beat.

Gwen   You won't let me go, will you, Colin?

Colin   No, Gwen, I won't.

Gwen   Not ever.

Colin   Not ever.

Gwen *comes to nestle under his arm, safe. Gazes out.*

In **Audrey***'s hotel room, there is muted music and laughter, rising up
from the bar. As* **Audrey** *waits for the future, she speak-sings softly:*

Audrey   You put your left arm in . . . your left arm out . . .
In . . . out . . . in . . . out . . . you shake it . . . all about . . .

The song continues under:

Gwen   Could be a desert here one day, Audrey said. Abu
Dhabi was green once. Y'can't believe it, can you?

Colin *doesn't respond.*

Gwen   Christmas soon.

Colin   Yeah.

Gwen That's something t'look forward to.

Gwen *and* **Colin** *look down the valley towards the river.*

After a while, **Colin** *breaks away from* **Gwen***, goes to his case. He snaps the airline luggage ticket off the handle. Fiddles with it, absorbed.*

Gwen *watches him for a moment, then goes back to looking out of the window. The lights on them fade gradually during the next scene.*

22

Mary *hurries into* **Alan***'s shop, the bell clanging brightly over the door. She's carrying a large brown paper bag. She unpacks another bag from it, and then something else which she proffers to* **Alan***.*

Alan What's that?

Mary Ice lolly.

Alan In this weather?

Mary It's what I fancied.

Alan *takes it and* **Mary** *busies herself with the secret contents of the other bag.* **Alan** *takes off the lolly wrapper. The lolly is an incredibly unnatural bright blue.*

Alan What flavour's this?

Mary *looks round.*

Mary Blue.

Alan What's in it?

Mary Science. Don't eat it if you don't want it.

Alan *sucks on the lolly.*

Alan I hate it when the clocks go back.

Mary Why?

Alan Feels late.

Mary Yeah, but it's not.

Mary *turns to reveal two lighted sparklers.*

Alan   It's not bonfire night yet . . .

Mary   Hey, Alan . . . look at this . . . look – hey, Alan, look at me . . . are you looking . . . ?

She starts to turn slowly on the spot, the sparklers in her outstretched hands.

Hey, turn the light out . . .

Alan *watches her for a moment, spinning at greater speed now.*

Then he goes to the wall, takes down the picture of Steven, puts it in the drawer. He turns out the light, watches as **Mary** *spins, faster and faster, her head thrown back, the sparklers making a circle of flame trail around her. Beautiful.*

Mary   Hey, Alan, look . . .

Her excitement drifts into ecstasy.

Oh! Fuck – fuck me . . . fuck me!

The sparklers burn down to blackout.

Printed in the United Kingdom
by Lightning Source UK Ltd.
126014UK00001B/26/A